The No-Cry Nap Solution

As usual, Elizabeth Pantley has married solid research, advice, and support in one easy-to-understand book. She lays out the importance of naps, outlines many solutions, and then lets parents determine the best course of action based on their particular child. Parents of children from newborn to school age will find valuable information and advice in *The No-Cry Nap Solution*.

> —Kathy Lynn, president,
> Parenting Today,
> www.parentingtoday.ca

No one understands the significance of the nap better than parenting guru Elizabeth Pantley. Her clear and helpful writing and abundance of ideas will guide parents and children to calmer and more peaceful days.

> —Nancy Massotto, Ph.D., executive director,
> Holistic Moms Network,
> www.holisticmoms.org

I have counseled thousands of families and raised five children of my own, yet *The No-Cry Nap Solution* taught me things I was not expecting about the dynamics of sleep and, more important, what we as parents can do to help children get the rest that they need.

> —Maureen A. Doolan Boyle, executive director,
> MOST (Mothers of Supertwins), Inc.,
> www.MOSTonline.org,
> www.PreemieCare.org

Elizabeth Pantley's wise and warm writing style is as comforting as the sleep children will get if parents put her advice to use. She smoothly presents essential strategies and offers real-life scenarios. As she does in her previous books, Pantley comes through like a trusted friend, albeit one with words full of fairy dust to help little ones get the rest they need.

—*Gregory Keer, syndicated columnist and publisher of FamilyManOnline.com*

Elizabeth Pantley's gentle yet effective approach helps parents identify the causes of sleep problems and provides practical step-by-step solutions. Her ingenious Nap Plan and Hush Hour are a dream come true for parents with babies and children who resist napping.

—*Azmina Hansraj, editor, www.baby-mates.com, London, United Kingdom*

Parents and children from all over the world, from all walks of life, contributed to this book to give us a worldview into an issue that has a major impact on optimal functioning of your child, your household, your sanity, and your life.

—*Jolene Ivey, cofounder of Mocha Moms, www.mochamoms.org, and Maryland state delegate, www.JoleneIvey.com*

Elizabeth Pantley promotes a gentle, child-centered approach to solving sleep problems. The solutions are *relationship building*, an aspect that many child care books do not adequately address. The ideas are simple, natural, and hopeful.

—*Joan van Niekerk, national coordinator, Childline South Africa*

Elizabeth Pantley provides solutions and encourages parents to "work *with* their child" to find the best solution rather than advocating a "do *to* their child" approach that is so popular in other parenting books. It is wonderful to have another fantastic book by Elizabeth to recommend to parents.

—*Sally Cameron-Zurich, midwife, nurse, mother, and co-owner of Earth Babies, www.earthbabies.co.za*

The No-Cry Nap Solution covers a lot of territory, yet Elizabeth Pantley's easy style makes the content flow smoothly. This is a book filled with sensible, professional, and accessible advice for all parents and caregivers.

—*Neala Schwartzberg, Ph.D., editor of* Parent & Preschooler Newsletter

Elizabeth Pantley takes a positive, problem-solving approach to assisting parents in helping their babies and small children get the sleep they need. Elizabeth encourages parents to tune in to their children and assess their needs, rather than taking a cookie-cutter approach full of "shoulds" and "musts." She then offers an array of practical, effective strategies.

—*Barbara Glare, IBCLC,*
former president of ABA and counselor at
Australian Breastfeeding Association

This is a valuable tool for anyone who cares for children. This book is packed full of extremely useful methods. To have it at your fingertips is a must, and it will likely be used over and over again.

—*Lyndsey Garrett, editor and founder,*
Nanny's Helping Hand Magazine,
www.nannyshelpinghand.com

the no-cry nap solution

Guaranteed Gentle Ways to Solve All Your Naptime Problems

Elizabeth Pantley

New York Chicago San Francisco Lisbon London Madrid Mexico City
Milan New Delhi San Juan Seoul Singapore Sydney Toronto

Library of Congress Cataloging-in-Publication Data

Pantley, Elizabeth.
    The no-cry nap solution : guaranteed gentle ways to solve all your naptime problems /
by Elizabeth Pantley.
        p. cm.
    ISBN-13: 978-0-07-159695-4 (alk. paper)
    ISBN-10: 0-07-159695-X (alk. paper)
    1. Sleep disorders in children.   2. Children—Sleep.   3. Infants—Sleep.   4. Naps
(Sleep).   5. Parent and child.   6. Child rearing.   I. Title.

RJ506.S55P355   2009
618.92'8498—dc22   2008022973

1 2 3 4 5 6 7 8 9 10 11 12 13 14 15 16 17 18 19 20 21 22 23   DOC/DOC   0 9 8

ISBN 978-0-07-159695-4
MHID   0-07-159695-X

Illustrations on page 194 courtesy of Dr. Harvey Karp, author and creator of the book, CD,
and DVD *The Happiest Baby on the Block*, www.thehappiestbaby.com. Illustrations copyright
© 2002 by Jennifer Kalis.

McGraw-Hill books are available at special quantity discounts to use as premiums and sales
promotions or for use in corporate training programs. To contact a representative, please visit
the Contact Us pages at www.mhprofessional.com.

This book provides a variety of ideas and suggestions. It is sold with the understanding
that the publisher and author are not rendering psychological, medical, or professional
services. The author is not a doctor or psychologist, and the information in this book is the
author's opinion unless otherwise stated. Questions and comments attributed to parents
represent a compilation and adaptation of reader letters and test parent letters. This material
is presented without any warranty or guarantee of any kind, express or implied, including
but not limited to implied warranties of merchantability or fitness for a particular purpose.
It is not possible to cover every eventuality in any book, and the reader should consult a
professional for individual needs. Readers should bring their child to a medical care provider
for regular checkups and bring questions they have to a medical professional. This book is
not a substitute for competent professional health care or professional counseling.

Readers should be certain of their child's safety during naps. To review a complete set of
safety checklists for all sleeping conditions, please see the author's website at www.pantley
.com/elizabeth or the author's previous books *The No-Cry Sleep Solution* and *The No-Cry
Sleep Solution for Toddlers and Preschoolers*.

This book is printed on acid-free paper.

THIS BOOK IS DEDICATED TO YOU, DEAR READER.
I feel a special connection between us. I suspect that we are very much alike and that if we met, we would probably be friends. We are connected by our love for our children, a powerful emotion that parallels nothing else in our lives. We are connected by our worries and doubts that are so much a part of that love. And we are connected by our commitment to do the best job that we can as we raise our children.

I have dedicated my previous books to my husband, my four children, my mother, and my sisters, all the people I love most in the world. When I pondered to whom I should dedicate this new book, I thought immediately of you, because you trust me to help you as you raise your precious little one. I promise you that I take your trust very seriously.

Since you've chosen this book, I believe that we share core values by which we make our parenting decisions, such as kindness, respect, and gentleness. I also suspect that you agree with me that problems are meant to be solved, and not lived, and that what it takes is finding the right solution.

It is my sincere hope that you will find the answers here that you came for. It is my wish that this book will uplift you, support you, and even entertain you. And of course, I hope that by the time you finish this book, all your napping problems will be solved!

With warm wishes and hugs to you!

Contents

Foreword

We forge a connection with our children before they are born, and it lasts a lifetime. As parents, we are there as they give their first smile, speak their first words, and take their first steps, and together we mark the milestones in their journey toward adulthood.

Life with children is not always easy. We get to share their sleepless nights; times of pain, sickness, fussiness, temper tantrums, and squabbles; and the many other challenges of being a parent. Don't we all wish children came with a user's manual?

Elizabeth Pantley's books for parents are as close to a user's manual as there is. Her No-Cry books offer remarkably clear and practical advice. This latest book in the series addresses an issue we have all faced and many have struggled with: helping our children to nap.

Sleep is vitally important, especially to infants and young children. Just like with adults, sleep gives their growing bodies rest and recovery. Furthermore, it allows their young minds to process and integrate the sensory impressions and experiences of the day. Sleep is essential for both physical well-being and mental health.

Many children will drift off to sleep easily when they are tired or if they are overwhelmed with sensory impressions. Others are resistant. They may need excessive assistance from a parent. They may be unable to tune out distractions. They may not want to miss out on "all the fun," or they may not want to feel that they are being treated like a "baby." Some children are extremely sensitive to touch, irritation on their skin, or the slightest noise. Yet others find the issue of taking a nap to be a great way to assert their independence and resistance to our authority. Every child is different, and every family faces a unique set of challenges.

In *The No-Cry Nap Solution*, Elizabeth once again gives parents the tools to identify and understand their child's issues. She then provides varied yet specific solutions to their individual problems. She offers many ways that parents can help their babies and young children settle down to a daily rest—without tears, stress, or power struggles. Many parents will find the ideas solve their child's nighttime sleep problems, as well.

Elizabeth's insights and practical strategies have helped countless parents around the world. Her ideas are easy to adopt in your home because they are based on common sense, science, and the wisdom of experience. She deserves our thanks for providing reassurance and everyday advice and for helping us to become more effective as parents. She inspires us to build homes filled with warmth, love, kindness, and respect.

—Tim Seldin
President of the Montessori Foundation
Chair of the International Montessori Council
Author of *How to Raise an Amazing Child*

Acknowledgments

I would like to express my heartfelt appreciation to the many people who lift me up with their support every day, in so many ways:

Judith McCarthy, my awe-inspiring editor, and the entire amazing team of people at McGraw-Hill who help to create my books: after eight books together, still absolutely the best publisher ever.

Meredith Bernstein, of Meredith Bernstein Literary Agency: counselor, friend, and literary agent extraordinaire.

Patti "the Wonderful" Hughes: my incredible, enthusiastic, and loveable assistant.

My husband, Robert: my partner, my friend, and my soul mate for twenty-five blissful years and counting.

My family, my ultimate source of joy and inspiration: Mom, Angela, Vanessa, David, Coleton, Michelle, Loren, Sarah, Nicholas, Renée, Tom, Amber, Matthew, Devin, Tyler, and Wyatt.

All the readers who have written to me about their precious children; I feel a special friendship with each and every person who writes.

The many test mommies, test daddies, and test children, for sharing a piece of their lives with me: Abby, Abigail, Adeleine, Adrienne, Ainslee, Alesasia, Alex, Alexa, Alexander, Alicia, Alinah, Aliyah, Alyson, Alyssa, Amanda, Amelia, Ami, Ana, Analiese, Anamaria, Anastasia, Andea, André, Andrea, Andrew, Andy, Angela, Aniseh, Ann, Anna, Ann-Marie, Anthony, Archie, Ariana, Arianna, Ariella, Arran, Ashton, Audra, Austin, Autumn, Ava, Avery, Barbara, Barrett, Becky, Benjamin, Beth, Bethany, Bonnie, Brandel, Brandi, Brandy, Bridget, Brittany, Bryan, Byron, Caitlyn, Callen, Callie, Candace, Canon, Cara, Carlie, Carmella, Caroline, Carrie, Carter, Cashton, Casper,

Cathy, Catriona, Cayden, Charlene, Charlie, Charlotte, Cherene, Cheryl, Christi, Christine, Christopher, Clay, Cole, Colleen, Connor, Constanze, Cornelia, Cortney, Courtney, Daniel, Danielle, Dara, David, Dean, Debbie, Derryn, Diana, Doreen, Dovi, Drew, Dylan, Elena, Elijah, Elissa, Elizabeth, Ellen, Ellie, Emerson, Emily, Emma, Emmy, Emre, Ethan, Eva, Evan, Faith, Finn, Fiona, Frost, Gaia, Genevieve, Georgiana, Ginger, Gloria, Grace, Grayson, Hanna, Hannah, Heather, Hector, Heidi, Helena, Holden, Hollie, Holly, Hugh, Ian, Ilkim, Isabella, Jack, Jackson, Jacob, Jaelyn, James, Jamie, Jana, Janie, Jared, Jason, Jayden, Jayson, Jean, Jean-Luc, Jeannie, Jeni, Jennifer, Jenny, Jeremy, Jessie, Jill, Joann, Jody, Joel, Johari, John, Jon, Jonah, Jordan, Jordana, Joseph, Jubal, Jude, Julia, Jullian, Justine, Kaiden, Kalina, Kami, Kamryn, Kara, Karen, Kathi, Kathleen, Kathryn, Katy, Kayla, Keiran, Kelly, Kenderick, Kendra, Kerri, Khalid, Kieran, Kim, Kiran, Kirin, Kirstin, Kristen, Kristi, Kristin, Krystal, Kyle, Lana, Lara, Larissa, Laura, Lauren, Leah, Leila, Leilah, Leon, Leta, Liam, Lillian, Lindsey, Liora, Lisa, Loraine, Loralie, Lori, Lorrie, Lucy, Lucy Ann, Luke, Lynn, Mac Robert, Maddison, Madeline, Madison, Malachi, Manal, Margaret, Maria, Marisa, Marissa, Mark, Marsha, Mary, Mason, Matthew, Maureen, Maverick, Max, Maya, Meaghan, Meara, Megan, Melanie, Melissa, Mella, Michaela, Micheal, Michele, Michelle, Miguel, Mikayla, Mike, Miles, Miranda, Mordechai, Moshe, Nadine, Natalia, Natalie, Natasha, Nathan, Nathaniel, Negras, Neve, Nicholas, Nicola, Nicolas, Nicole, Nina, Noah, Noelia, Norman, Ocean, Oliva, Oliver, Olivia, Orion, Orit, Owen, Pamela, Parker, Patrick, Patti, Paul, Peri, Pnina, Preston, Pyrra, Quinton, Rachel, Reagan, Rebecca, Rebekah, Renee, Rhyann, Riley, Robert, Ruxandra, Ryan, Sakina, Sam, Samantha, Samuel, Sandi, Sandra, Sarah, Savannah, Scarlett, Schaefer, Sebastian, Şebnem, September, Shannon, Shari, Sharon, Shauna, Shellie, Sidney, Sierra, Silias, Siobhan, Skylan, Sloan, Sofia, Spencer, Stacey, Stacy, Stephanie, Stevan, Steven, Susan, Tahlia, Tami, Tammy, Tara, Taylor, Tessa, Thatcher, Theresa, Thomas, Tina, Tobias, Tonya, Tracey, Tyler,

Vaughn, Veronica, Vicki, Wendy, Will, William, Xander, Yedidya, Yonina, Zachary, Zanon, and Zoë.

The Test Parents

During the creation of this book, I received input, ideas, questions, and glorious photos from an incredible group of test parents. These 209 people let me peek into their families' napping problems and happy successes.

The No-Cry test parents live all over the world, and they represent all different kinds of families: married, single, unmarried partners, from one child up to five children, twins, triplets, adopted children, young parents, older parents, at-home moms, at-home dads, working parents, interracial families, multicultural families, gay families, and one grandparent-as-parent. The Test Mommies and Daddies, as I affectionately call them, became my friends during this long and complicated process, and I believe I learned as much from them as they learned from me. They are a varied and interesting group, as you can see.

Locations
- **152 from the United States:** Alabama, Arizona, California, Colorado, Connecticut, Florida, Idaho, Illinois, Indiana, Iowa, Kansas, Maine, Maryland, Massachusetts, Michigan, Minnesota, Missouri, Montana, North Carolina, Nebraska, New Jersey, New York, New Mexico, Ohio, Oklahoma, Oregon, Pennsylvania, Rhode Island, South Carolina, South Dakota, Texas, Utah, Virginia, Washington, West Virginia, Wisconsin, Wyoming
- **22 from Canada:** Alberta, Battleford, Calgary, Chatham, Etobicoke, Guelph, Manitoba, Ontario, Ottawa, Ramea, Saskatoon, Sturgeon Falls, Thompson, Tisdale, Victoria, Winnipeg

- **1 from Greece:** Athens
- **1 from Turkey:** Beşiktaş
- **4 from New Zealand:** Hibiscus Coast, Lower Hutt, Wainuiomata, Wellington
- **1 from Germany:** Filderstadt
- **8 from the United Kingdom:** Devon, East Sussex, Hook, Kent, London, Peterborough, Suffolk
- **1 from Italy:** Varese
- **1 from Spain:** Soto de la Marina
- **1 from Norway:** Vikersund
- **1 from Cyprus:** Limassol
- **6 from Australia:** Albion Park, Flagstaff Hill, Tarragindi, Queensland, Terrigal, Victoria
- **2 from South Africa:** Cresta, Sandton
- **2 from Saudi Arabia:** Al Hassa, Dubai
- **1 from Scotland:** Kinross
- **3 from Israel:** Jerusalem, Nof Ayalon, Tel-Aviv
- **1 from The Netherlands:** Harderwijk
- **1 from Slovenia:** Maribor

Children

- 118 girls
- 155 boys
- 6 sets of twins
- 1 set of triplets
- 134 infants (birth to 12 months)
- 82 toddlers (12 months up to 3 years)
- 41 preschoolers (3 years to 6 years)
- 20 children (7 years to 10 years)

A Word from a Sleep Doctor

Sleep is as essential to life as is breathing, eating, and drinking. It is absolutely critical to human existence. Our children's bodies do not shut down when they sleep. Sleep is not like turning off a computer. It is a time when energy is restored, bodily functions are renovated, and damaged tissues are repaired. When children sleep, hormones (especially those related to growth) are secreted, breathing and the heart are controlled, the functions of organs continue, memories are stored, and dreams occur. When children don't sleep, or don't sleep enough, many things can go wrong. Examples include being so sleepy that they cannot learn or function normally, or having abnormal hormone function, which may predispose them to obesity and diabetes. At a minimum, a shortage of proper sleep can cause a disruption to mood and behavior.

How much children sleep, when they sleep, and how much deep sleep and dreaming sleep they need varies with age. What is often forgotten with infants and young children is that an essential part of the amount of daily sleep they need occurs during the daytime. We call these *naps*, and they are extremely important. Indeed, they are vital to the health and welfare of the very young.

In this book, Elizabeth Pantley explains to readers why naps are important, describes how they can make a difference in a child's and the family's life, and gives important lessons to parents on how to help their children nap the right amount to maximize their well-being. Elizabeth gives advice on how to handle many types of napping problems. She recognizes that every child is different, and what may work for one child may not work for another. She explains that sleep patterns change tremendously in the early years of life and helps parents to identify and deal with these changes. Elizabeth defines and explains all the common problems and offers many solutions.

Understanding the facts about the importance of naps is only the first step. Parents must find ways to decipher the best nap schedules for their children and then convince them to sleep on this schedule. Elizabeth covers both the whys and hows in precise detail. She has a wonderful ability to communicate what is important about a topic that is vital for the development, health, and well-being of your child.

Meir Kryger, M.D.
Director of Research and Education,
Gaylord Sleep Medicine
Chairman of the Board, National Sleep Foundation
Author of *A Woman's Guide to Sleep Disorders* (2004)
and *A Good Night's Sleep* (2009)

Part 1

Nap Magic

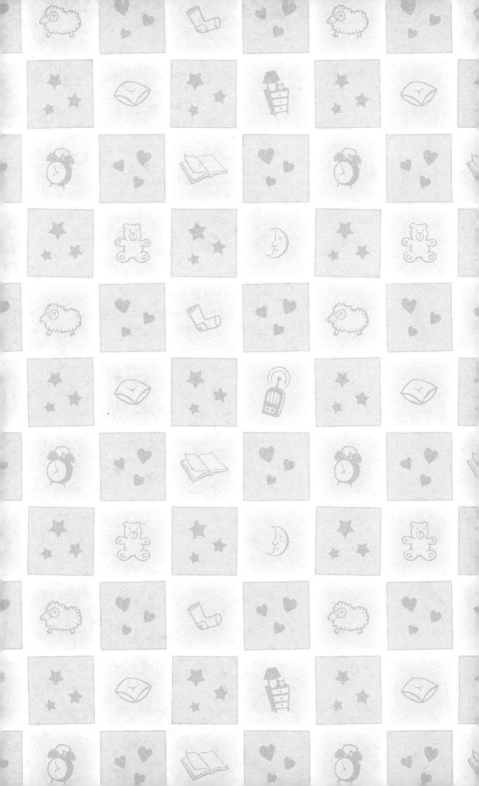

Naps

The Key to a Happy, Healthy Child

Naps take only a few hours of time, but they shape all *twenty-four* hours of your child's day. The quality and quantity of your child's naps influence his mood, behavior, health, and brain development. Naps can affect how cheerful your child is when she wakes up in the morning, whether or not she whines, fusses, and has tantrums all day, and how easily she'll go to bed at night. An appropriate nap schedule is a vital component for your child's healthy, happy life. When you consider all of this, you'll understand that your child's naps—or lack of naps—can affect all twenty-four hours of *your* day as well as your child's.

I thought I knew everything there was to know about naps, since I've written two other books and countless articles about children and sleep, but I was shocked and amazed at the new information I discovered while writing this book. I set out on this venture knowing that parents struggle getting their children to nap; it's a frequent topic that readers write to me about. Everyone knows that children need naps, but the biological reasons behind this will convince you, without a doubt, that you should do everything you can to provide your child with daily naptime. It is common knowledge that when a child misses a nap, he gets cranky, but you will be intrigued to learn the actual reasons why this happens. So, before we delve into typical nap problems and a plethora of ways to solve them, let's explore the background information that will provide an understanding and foundation for all the solutions that follow.

Naps: What Is the Magic?

A nap is a miraculous, life-enhancing activity. A nap can transform a crying, fussing baby into a cooing, smiling delight. A nap can convert a cranky, whiny child into a happier, healthier, and more adaptable little person. A nap can rescue a grouchy, moody parent and allow the loving mom or dad to reappear. Naps are magical breaks in the day that rejuvenate the entire family.

> **Key Point**
> Science proves what parents instinctually know: *naps are absolutely necessary.*

Napping is an important component of a child's healthy mental, physical, and social growth. Naps boost energy, focus, and the ability to learn. Naps benefit a child in a number of ways.

- **Naps are a biological necessity.** Children have natural dips in energy during the day, even after a full night's sleep. A lack of response to this natural craving for rest results in a biological misfiring that leads to behavioral, emotional, and physical problems. Naps that correspond with energy dips allow the body and mind to function properly.
- **Naps reduce the day's fussiness, whining, and tantrums.** A midday nap enables the body to release cortisol and other hormones that combat stress and tension. Without the release of these hormones, they build to uncontrollable levels and create inner pressure that erupts as unpleasant behavior. Children who do not get enough sleep have difficulty controlling their emotions. High-need children or those with more intense, active personalities can have an exaggerated effect from sleep shortages. Daily naps can be a lifeline for them and their families.

- **Naps increase learning capacity for babies.** Babies who have adequate naps spend more of their waking hours in a relaxed, alert condition. They learn more, they enjoy life more, and their parents are provided with added quality time for engaging, teaching, and bonding with their babies.
- **Naps fill gaps from poor nighttime sleep.** Napping can help a child recover from problems in the prior night's sleep. Any shortage of night sleep is damaging to your child's health and behavior, so naps are a critically important way for children to make up for less than a perfect night's sleep. Surprisingly, children who *do* sleep well at night receive as much benefit from naps as their night-waking peers, since nap sleep is different from night sleep in its configuration of sleep cycles and in its effect on a child's health and behavior. Extra night sleep doesn't achieve the same results as a good night's sleep *plus* naps.
- **Naps improve a child's mood.** A child is typically happier following a daytime snooze, which is as good for the parent as it is for the child. Naptime can stabilize a child's mood over the course of the day, eliminating the frustrating highs and lows of mood swings and crankiness.
- **Naps improve brain development.** Adequate sleep is crucial to proper brain development. Napping plays a role in learning by helping to convert new information into a permanent place in the memory. Naps allow a child midday pauses to store new information and make room for the remainder of the day's learning. Sufficient sleep is also thought to help young brains develop the ability to achieve high levels of abstract thinking.
- **Naps improve the bedtime routine.** A child who needs a nap but doesn't get one will get overtired throughout the day yet become hyperactive and resist the idea of bedtime when it arrives. An overtired child may find it difficult to fall asleep at bedtime.
- **Naps increase attention span.** Children who nap have longer attention spans and are better able to absorb new information. Conversely, children who lack appropriate sleep tend to be less

focused, so much so that researchers believe that over 20 percent of children diagnosed with hyperactivity disorders such as attention deficit hyperactivity disorder (ADHD) are actually suffering from sleep disorders.

- **Naps ensure proper growth and development.** Growth hormone is released during deep sleep, and children who sleep well are assured their necessary sleep-assisted growth. Naps provide a child's body with downtime needed for rejuvenation and repair. Naps also fuel the dramatic developmental surges that occur when children learn to master major physical and mental milestones.
- **Children's naps give caregivers a needed break.** No matter how much they love and adore them, adults sometimes need their little ones to nap just as much as their children need the nap. During naptime, caregivers can reenergize, do a few things for themselves, or handle tasks that cannot be done when tending to children. A nap break relieves adult stress and assures that caregivers can enjoy their little nappers more when they wake up.
- **Naps are beneficial for people of all ages.** There is no time when your child must—or should—give up naps. Naps are healthy for all human beings. Even fervent nonnappers can learn

 Research Report

Researchers at the University of Michigan found that third graders need a minimum of nine hours and forty-five minutes of sleep each night to lower their risk of obesity. Sleeping more than this minimum amount lowered their risk even more—by up to 40 percent. "The less sleep they got, the more likely the children were to be obese in sixth grade, no matter what the child's weight was in third grade," said Dr. Julie Lumeng, who led the research.

to embrace the idea of naps and enjoy the many physical, emotional, and social benefits that they bring.

How Much Naptime Does Your Child Need?

The actual number of hours that your child sleeps is an incredibly important factor for his health and well-being. A sleep study completed by Dr. Avi Sadeh at Tel Aviv University demonstrated that even a *one-hour* shortage in appropriate sleep time will compromise a child's alertness and brain functioning and increase fatigue. Dr. William C. Dement, known as the world's leading authority on sleep, takes that one step further and says, ". . . the effects of delaying bedtime by even *half an hour* can be subtle and pernicious [very destructive]." These are amazing findings and call for us to look very closely at the total number of hours our children are sleeping. Every child is unique and has his own "personal best" amount of sleep. Your child's behavior, mood, and health can give you an indication if he is getting the right amount of sleep. If you suspect that your child may not be sleeping enough and if your child is not getting *close to* the amount of sleep on the following chart, he may be "chronically overtired," and this will directly affect his behavior, moods, health, learning, and growth.

As you will learn in the next section, the length of time that your child is awake from one sleep period to the next will also have a powerful impact on his temperament and behavior, so it is one more important consideration and earns a prominent place on the chart. You'll see that the span of awake time is very, *very* short for a newborn baby and this gradually increases over time.

This sleep chart is an important guide to your child's sleep hours. All children are different, and a few truly do need less (or more) sleep than shown here, but the vast majority of children have sleep needs that fall within the range shown on this chart.

Sleep Chart: Average Hours of Daytime and Nighttime Sleep

Age	Number of Naps	Total Hours of Naptime Sleep	Endurable Awake Hours Between Sleep Periods	Total Hours of Nighttime Sleep*	Total Hours of Nap and Night Sleep**
Newborn***			1–2		
1 month	3–4	6–7	1–3	8½–10	15–16
3 months	3–4	5–6	2–3	10–11	15
6 months	2–3	3–4	2–3	10–11	14–15
9 months	2	2½–4	2–4	11–12	14
12 months	1–2	2–3	3–4	11½–12	13½–14
18 months	1–2	2–3	4–6	11¼–12	13–14
2 years	1	1½–3	5–6½	11–12	13–13½
3 years	1	1–2	6–8	11–11½	12–13
4 years	0–1	0–2	6–12	11–11½	11½–12½
5 years	0–1	0–2	6–12	11	11–12
6 years	0–1	0–2	6–13	10½–11	10–11
10 years	0–1	0–2****	8–14	10	10
17 years	0–1	0–3****	8–16	8½–10	8½–10
Adult	0–1	0–1½****	8–16	7–9	7–9

*These are averages and do not necessarily represent unbroken stretches of sleep, since brief awaking between sleep cycles is normal.
**The hours shown don't always add up, because when children take longer naps, they may sleep fewer hours at night and vice versa.
***Newborns sleep fifteen to eighteen hours, distributed over four to seven sleep periods. Premature or sick babies may sleep more hours divided into more sleep periods.
****Older children, teenagers, and adults often nap to catch up on a shortage of nighttime hours.

The No-Cry Nap Solution © Better Beginnings, Inc.

Important Facts You Should Know About Sleep

When we think of sleep, we visualize a quiet child at rest, doing nothing. Actually, sleep is a complex process that is far from passive. It provides your child with the mental, emotional, and physical fuel needed to function each and every day. Sleep is a dynamic activity—a complex series of phases, each of which makes important contributions to health and well-being. The following chart shows the various stages of sleep and describes what happens at each phase.

Stages of Sleep

Stage of Sleep	Description	Depth of Sleep	Physical and Mental States/Processes
Presleep	Drowsy	Depending on conditions, can move into Stage 1 or get a second wind and become wide awake	Relaxed
Stage 1	Drifting off, very light sleep	Falling asleep, easily awakened	Floating sensation, relaxed muscles; slower heart rate and breathing; body may make a sudden jerking motion
Stage 2	Light to moderate sleep	Easily awakened	Regular, relaxed breathing; preparing to enter deep sleep

continued

Stages of Sleep, *continued*

Stage of Sleep	Description	Depth of Sleep	Physical and Mental States/Processes
Stage 3	Deep sleep	Difficult to awaken	Regular, relaxed breathing; bed-wetting, night terrors, sleepwalking, or sleep talking may occur
Stage 4	Deepest sleep	Very difficult to awaken; groggy or disoriented when awakened	Slow and regular breathing; no muscle activity; bed-wetting, night terrors, sleepwalking, or sleep talking may occur
REM stage	Dreaming	May be easy or difficult to awaken	Large muscles immobile; small muscles twitch; heart and breathing rates increase; eyes move quickly (REM stands for rapid eye movement)
Sleep inertia	Awakening	The transition between sleep and complete wakefulness; may fall back to sleep or wake up fully	May act groggy, disoriented, or confused; reaction time and performance can be hindered

Note: Each of the first four stages of sleep lasts from 5 to 15 minutes, and a complete cycle of the five stages of sleep takes between 90 and 120 minutes. Stages 2 and 3 actually repeat backward before dreaming sleep is entered, so the sleep cycle actually looks like this: Drowsy, Stage 1, 2, 3, 4, 3, REM, 2, 3, 4, 3, 2, REM—continuing by alternating between REM and non-REM sleep in a cyclical pattern. Infants can fall asleep directly into REM sleep. Infant sleep cycles last approximately 40 to 60 minutes.

Why Short Catnaps Are Not Good Enough

If your child's naps are shorter than an hour and a half in length, you might suspect that these catnaps aren't meeting your child's sleep needs—and you would be right. A short nap takes the edge off but doesn't offer the physical and mental nourishment that a

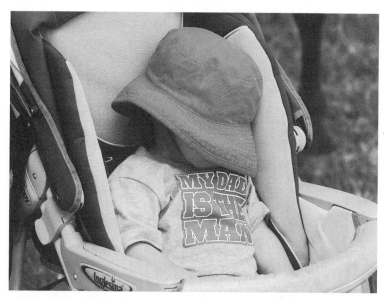

Keiran, fourteen months old

longer nap provides. (If your child is a catnapper, you can find solutions in the chapter "Catnaps: Making Short Naps Longer.")

As shown in the chart, it takes between 90 and 120 minutes for your child to move through one sleep cycle. Each stage of sleep brings a different benefit to the sleeper. Imagine, if you will, magic gifts that are awarded at each new stage of sleep. In order for your child to receive all of these wonderful gifts, he must sleep long enough to pass through each stage.

Newborn babies have unique cycles that mature over time. A newborn sleep cycle is about forty to sixty minutes long, and an infant enters dream sleep quickly, skipping several stages. By the time a baby is six to eight months old, his sleep will have become more organized into the cycle pattern. (Newborn sleep is explained beginning on page 35.)

The following chart lists the benefits of a complete nap. It shows the "magic gifts" to be had during each stage of the sleep cycle.

Benefits Derived at Each Stage of the Sleep Cycle

	Stage of Sleep	Description	Approximate Length of Time*	Benefits of Stage
	Presleep	Drowsy	Varies	Prepares body for sleep Reduces feelings of sleepiness
	Stage 1	Drifting off, very light sleep	5 to 15 minutes	
	Stage 2	Light to moderate sleep	5 to 15 minutes	Increases alertness Improves motor skills Stabilizes mood Slightly reduces homeostatic sleep pressure
	Stage 3	Deep sleep	5 to 15 minutes	Strengthens memory and immune system Releases growth hormone Repairs bones, tissues, and muscles Regulates appetite Releases stress and restores energy Reduces homeostatic sleep pressure
	Stage 4	Deepest sleep	5 to 15 minutes	Same benefits as Stage 3, but enhanced
	Return to Stage 3	Deep sleep	3 to 10 minutes	Same as Stage 3 above
	Return to Stage 2	Light to moderate sleep	3 to 10 minutes	Same as Stage 2 above

First REM stage**	Dreaming	9 to 30 minutes	Transfers short-term memory to long-term Secures new learning Enhances brain connections Sharpens visual and perceptual skills Processes emotions and relieves stress Inspires creativity and boosts energy Reduces homeostatic sleep pressure
Stage 2	Light to moderate sleep	5 to 15 minutes	Same as Stage 2 above
Stage 3	Deep sleep	5 to 15 minutes	Same as Stage 3 above
Stage 4	Deepest sleep	5 to 15 minutes	Same as Stage 4 above
Stage 3	Deep sleep	5 to 15 minutes	Same as Stage 3 above
Stage 2	Light to moderate sleep	5 to 15 minutes	Same as Stage 2 above
Second REM stage**	Dreaming	20 to 60 minutes	Same as REM stage above

*Add the minutes of each stage together for total naptime. The timing of each stage of sleep is unique to each nap, so times shown are approximations. In addition, sleep deprivation, medications, health issues, timing of the previous sleep session, and other factors can alter the cycle pattern. Infants have shorter sleep cycles than shown.

**The time spent in REM sleep increases with additional cycles. Infants spend more time in REM sleep than older babies and children, who have more REM sleep than adults.

Note: The same sequence applies to night sleep, resulting in five or more cycles per night and bringing that well-rested morning feeling.

The No-Cry Nap Solution © Better Beginnings, Inc.

Why the Timing of Naps Is Vitally Important

From the moment your child wakes in the morning, he is slowly using up the benefits of the previous night's sleep. He wakes up refreshed, but as the hours pass, little by little the benefits of his sleep time are used up, and an urge to return to sleep begins to build. When we catch a child at in-between stages and provide naps, we build up his reservoir of sleep-related benefits, allowing him a "fresh start" after each sleep period.

As shown on the sleep chart on page 8, as children age, the length of time that they can stay happily awake increases. A newborn can be awake only one or two hours before tiredness sets in, whereas a two-year-old can last five to seven hours before craving some downtime. When children are pushed beyond the time span that is ideal, biologically speaking, for them to be awake without a rest break, that's when they become fatigued and unhappy. As the day progresses and the sleep pressure builds, a child becomes fussier, whinier, and less flexible. He has more crying spells, more tantrums, and less patience. He loses concentration and the ability to learn new information. The scientific term for this process is "homeostatic sleep pressure" or "homeostatic sleep drive." I call it "the Volcano Effect." We've all seen the effects of this on a baby or child, as it is often as clear as watching a volcano erupt; nearly everyone has observed a fussy child and thought or said, "Someone needs a nap!"

As a child progresses through his day, his biology demands a nap so he can regroup. Without a nap break, the homeostatic pressure continues building until the end of the day, growing in intensity, so that a child becomes overtired, wired, and unable to stop the explosion. The result is an intense bedtime battle with a cranky, overtired child who won't fall asleep no matter how tired he is.

Even more, a child who misses naps day after day builds a sleep deprivation that launches her into the volcano stage much easier and quicker. If she is missing naps *and* lacking the appropriate nighttime sleep . . . watch out!

This concept brings to light one more important point: quality naps can make up for lost night sleep—but extra nighttime sleep does *not* make up for missed naps, as made clear by the homeostatic sleep pressure concept. Therefore, no matter how your child sleeps at night—great sleeper or poor sleeper—his daily naps are critically important to release the rising sleep pressure.

Infants have a much shorter span in which their sleep pressure builds. They rapidly reach the peak of their volcano in one to three hours. This is why newborns sleep throughout the day and why young babies require multiple naps. Over time as a baby's sleep cycle matures, he will be able to go longer periods between sleeps. It is not until age four or five that a child is able to go through the entire day without a nap, and research suggests that even through adulthood, a midday rest break is beneficial in reducing the pressure. The following charts represent the building and outcome of the Volcano Effect.

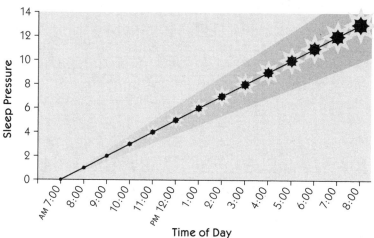

The Volcano Effect for a Child Without a Nap

The Volcano Effect for a Child with a Midday Nap

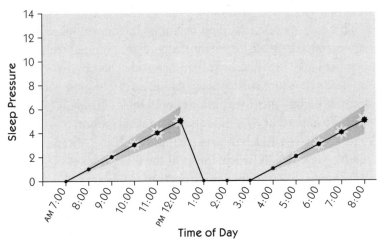

Time of Day

The Volcano Effect for a Child with Two Naps

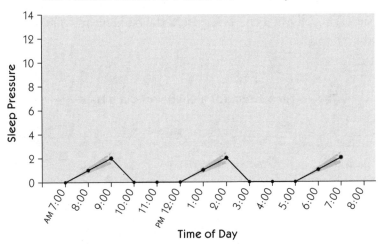

Time of Day

Is Anyone Else in the Family Affected by Homeostatic Sleep Pressure?

The Volcano Effect is not something reserved for children! This biological process affects adults as well. Understanding this can help you interpret what is really going on in your home at the end of a long day when children are fussy and parents are grumpy—resulting in a whole mountain range of volcanoes. What's more, each person's moodiness feeds off the others', causing contagious crankiness. You'll find yourself losing patience and saying to your child, "I'm sorry, honey. Mommy's just tired right now." (This is a very telling explanation we don't often stop to analyze.)

Homeostatic sleep pressure can tell us much about the time of day that is often referred to by names such as the "fussy hour," the "witching hour," or the more desperate (and, amusingly, most common) nickname, defined for us by Dictionary.com:

> **arsenic hour** (AR.suh.nik owur) *n.* the time of day when both children and parents have come home but dinner has not yet been served, seen as being difficult due to everyone being tired and hungry

When a daily nap routine is established, you may be delighted to find that you can avoid this daily meltdown and your evenings will become a more relaxed and pleasant time for all.

Avoiding Late-Day Naps

You can't force a child to be sleepy just because the clock says it is naptime. We all know what it's like to put a bright-eyed, wide-awake child in bed—there's no sleep to be had for anyone! However, it makes sense that the longer your child has been awake, the more tired he becomes. Sleepiness must build up to an ample level in order for your child to feel tired and fall asleep again. Therefore, you must allow enough time between sleep sessions to build up this pressure. This explains why a child resists a nap too soon after waking up in the morning and why a late nap too close to bedtime brings a bedtime battle.

Keep in mind that sleep pressure is not the only biological process affecting your child. The "magic gifts" are being given out all

Research Report

Studies completed at NASA of military pilots and astronauts found that naps improved working memory, performance, and alertness and offered a boost in mental sharpness. In general, they found that longer naps were better naps.

night long or all through a nap. If your child's sleep period has not been long enough, he won't wake up fully refreshed, at the bottom of his volcano. He will wake up somewhere in the middle or even toward the top. This explains the early-waking baby or short-napping child who is grumpy and fussy right from the moment he awakes. He hasn't received his full allotment of gifts—and he knows it!

The Biological Reason for the Second Wind

What happens if your child falls asleep, perhaps in the car or in your arms, for only five to fifteen minutes? He'll likely wake up appearing refreshed and full of energy and be unable to fall back to sleep. If you'll refer back to the "magic gifts" (sleep benefits) chart on page 12, you will see that the very first stage of sleep reduces feelings of sleepiness. Therefore this brief micro-nap has eliminated tiredness for the moment but has not allowed a child to gather his gifts from all the other sleep stages. One of those benefits is reducing his building sleep pressure, so the pressure is still there, just masked for a short time by the reduced feelings of fatigue. But as the day goes on, the mask is lifted to reveal a child more prone to frustration, fussing, crying, and temper tantrums.

What happens when you miss your child's tired signs entirely and ignore his building sleep pressure? Your child may end up falling asleep on his own in a soothing environment, such as while riding in the car, sitting in a swing, or lounging in front of the television, and catch his five or ten minutes, or he might take a long, late nap that interferes with bedtime. Or your child might pass over his tired spell and catch a second wind—without any sleep at all. Suddenly, he's filled with energy and action, as if he's had a double cappuccino! How can this be?

This no-sleep second wind occurs because your child has yet another system affecting his feelings of tiredness and alertness: his *circadian rhythm*, commonly called his *biological clock*. All human beings have this internal clock that regulates wakefulness and sleep. When it's working properly, we feel awake and alert during the day and sleepy at bedtime. Our clock easily resets itself each day based on our sleep habits, the timing of our meals, and our exposure to light and dark.

The biological clock functions separately from homeostatic sleep pressure, so even if sleep pressure is building, the timing of meals and the effects of activity and light can bring a child a whoosh of alertness even if he hasn't slowed down for a nap. However, sleep pressure is still there, hiding beneath the surface, and it continues to build. Later in the day—likely after dinner or during your prebedtime routine—your child will have a sudden drastic increase in fatigue, which causes battles with an exhausted child who, ironically, cannot fall asleep easily.

Some children have internal clocks that set easily; others have a finicky system that can be upset by a disruption in the nap schedule or any kind of external cue, such as lights or noises after they fall asleep or too early in the morning. Haphazard nap and bedtimes, irregular mealtimes, or too much activity before bedtime can skew a child's biological clock as well, disturbing his state of biochemical equilibrium and causing an inability to fall asleep, poor-quality sleep, an inability to nap, or too-early waking in the morning.

The human biological clock needs winding every day, and setting and keeping a daily naptime will help keep your child's biological clock working properly and in sync with his homeostatic sleep pressure so that his volcano need not erupt.

Night Sleep Versus Nap Sleep

Nap problems are often more of a challenge to solve than night sleep troubles. This is in part due to a more specific and intense need for night sleep. The need for a nap can be suppressed or overridden. In addition, lifestyle dictates nighttime sleep, but daytime naps can be avoided. The human body automatically craves sleep from about the time the sun sets to when it rises again. Naptime, however, doesn't have this very specific regulator, and nap needs are slightly different child by child and even day by day.

Even though it can be more complicated to manage, nap sleep is just as important to your child's health, behavior, and development as his nighttime sleep, so it is worth the effort to create and maintain a healthy napping routine.

Professional-Speak

"Sleep is one of your baby's most important jobs, and helping your baby sleep is one of *your* most important jobs as a parent."

—Dr. Polly Moore, Director of Sleep Research at
California Clinical Trials in San Diego

Naps: How and Where?

Now you know the answers to the question, *Why are naps critically important?* The answers to the "hows" and "wheres" are much more vague and flexible. As I am researching this book, I am amazed at the amount of "shoulds" I am coming across. You *should* do this.

You *must* do that. All types of professionals direct parents about how and where their child should nap, many with dire warnings should you fail to follow their advice.

When I blocked out all the noise and looked at the bottom-line results, it all boiled down to this: *there are no absolute rules that you must follow when it comes to where or how your child naps.* And in truth, following absolute rules that are presented as cookie-cutter solutions for all children will often fail you because each child is an individual with a distinctive personality and unique needs.

The Three Critical Nap Questions

There are three critical questions that need to be explored as you figure out the details of your child's sleep. The answers to them should be used as your guide to answer the "hows" and "wheres" of your child's naps. Once you've answered them, then you can proceed with your own unique best solutions.

There are no right answers. (No matter what anyone else tells you.) The best nap solutions are vastly different for every single child. The three critical questions that should guide your child's napping plan are these:

- Is my child getting enough sleep?
- Is the sleeping place safe?
- Is everyone in the household happy with the situation?

Solving Your Child's Napping Problems

This book is about solving those problems that *you* feel are problems. Just because there is a chapter about how to help your baby stop napping in your arms doesn't mean that napping in your arms is an evil sin to be banished and you must stop now no matter what—it means that *if* having your baby nap in your arms is a problem for *you*, then I will provide you with ideas that will help you make a change. Even within the group of parents wanting to move babies out of in-arms naps, each will find different solutions that work best for them, so I will provide an assortment of ideas for you to choose from for each situation.

With this important concept in mind, let's start with a crucial principle that I urge you to keep as a guiding light throughout the rest of this book and, for that matter, through the rest of your life:

 The No-Cry Process for Peaceful Problem Solving

There are no absolute rules about raising children and no guarantees for any parenting techniques. Raise your children how you choose to raise them and in ways that are right for you. Within the range of your comfort zone, modify your approach for each of your children based on their needs, personality, and temperament.

Address only those problems that are true problems to you, and don't create or imagine problems because someone else thinks you have them, no matter if that person is family, friend, or expert.

Keep your problems in perspective and take ample time to plot the best course of action. Solve your problems by analyzing possible solutions and choosing those solutions that are right for you and your family. Know that there is rarely one right answer, and often it will take multiple routes before getting to the best destination.

Read, listen, and learn constantly, but always sift what you learn through the strainer of your own personal beliefs and parenting philosophy.

Create Your Sleep Logs
and Your Nap Plan

When you begin to work on improving your child's naps, it can be helpful to pick one day and create logs to record your child's current sleeping patterns. These logs can help you analyze how your child is sleeping and will help you determine which ideas will best apply to your situation. The other advantage of doing these logs is that you'll have a baseline from which you can judge the effectiveness of your plan. By doing one new set of logs every month or two, you'll be able to see how your little one's nap routines are changing and thus be better able to make adjustments in your plan if you need to.

The logs are intended to help you through the process and should give you a feeling of control over what may now be an out-of-control situation. They are a tool to guide you. If, however, one look at them gives you hives, then by all means skip the logs and go directly on to creating your plan. If even making a plan seems like too much work, then just find the chapter that best defines your problem and use any ideas that sound right for you. The last thing I want to do is create any stress for you. Many parents find, however, that the logs help them to make clearer decisions about what needs to change. Don't be tempted to log any more frequently than every two to four weeks, though, as you might create unnecessary tension over sleep issues.

Create Your Sleep Logs

What follows are two logs: a *nap log* and a *daily schedule log*. Each one shows a sample entry. You will also find questions to help you

(cont. on p. 26)

Nap Log

Name: _____

Age: _____

Date: _____

Time child fell asleep and woke up*	How child fell asleep	Where child slept	How long child slept	Awake time from previous waking to this sleep time
7:00	Morning wake-up time			
10:00–11:30	Swaddled and swinging	In his swing	1 hour, 30 minutes	3 hours

*You may want to round numbers to make the chart easier to analyze.

Daily Schedule Log

Name: _____

Age: _____

Date: _____

Record these activities:

Wake up (in the morning and after naps)*
Eat (include meals and snacks)
Fall asleep (include naps and bedtime)

Time	Activity
7:00	Wake up

*If night waking is a problem, refer to the information about night sleep on my website at www.nocry sleepsolution.com.

evaluate your child's nap patterns and a worksheet to help you set a plan.

The *nap log* is important as it will show how long it takes your child to fall asleep, where and how he falls asleep, and when and how long he naps—which will all be valuable to analyze.

The *daily schedule log* will help you see how the rest of your child's day unfolds. This gives you a broader perspective, since other factors in your child's day will also affect his napping, and since his napping likely affects his night sleep and vice versa. These logs will direct you toward your best naptime solutions and help you monitor your progress.

Sleep Plan Questions

Take a minute to review the logs you've created, the chart of sleep hours on page 8, and the information in Part 1, "Nap Magic," and answer the following questions:

How many hours of nighttime sleep *should* your child be getting? _____

How many hours of nighttime sleep *is* your child getting now? _____

How many naps *should* your child be getting? _____

How many naps *is* your child getting now? _____

How many hours of daytime sleep (naps) *should* your child be getting? _____

How many hours of daytime sleep (naps) *is* your child getting now? _____

How many hours *should* your child be awake between getting up in the morning and the first nap? _____

How many hours *is* your child awake between getting up in the morning and the first nap? _____

How many hours *should* your child be awake between the first nap and the second nap? _____

How many hours *is* your child awake between the first nap and the second nap? _____

How many hours *should* your child be awake between the last nap of the day and bedtime? _____

How many hours *is* your child awake between the last nap of the day and bedtime? _____

How many total hours of sleep *should* your child be getting? _____

How many total hours of sleep *is* your child getting now? _____

How do the suggested hours of sleep on the chart compare to your child's actual hours of sleep?

Gets _____ hours *too little daytime* sleep

Gets _____ hours *too much daytime* sleep

Gets _____ hours *too little nighttime* sleep

Gets _____ hours *too much nighttime* sleep

Is your child frequently awake for too long between sleep periods? _____

Create a Nap Plan

Throughout this book you'll find a multitude of ideas that are subject-specific so you can choose those that suit your situation, your personality, and your family. Writing down your plan will consolidate all your ideas in one place for easy reference and will help you to remember the things you are going to do.

Even if you begin by making a few subtle changes, you may see *improvement* in your child's napping, so go ahead and begin using any ideas that make sense to you along the way, even before you settle on an exact plan. The sooner you get started, the better!

As you work though your plan, try to stay relaxed about it, but be consistent. Do give each idea enough time to have an impact—at least two or three weeks. A day or two isn't enough time to judge an idea's value. This is not a quick-fix plan, but it is a plan that will enable you to help your child become a healthy napper. After all, it has taken longer than a day or two to get where you are now, and habits take some time to change, not to mention that biology and maturity are part of the picture as well. Keep in mind that parenting isn't a sprint, it's a marathon, and you've only just begun, so there's no reason to rush yourself or your child.

You can copy and fill in the following pages or visit my website, www.nocrysleepsolution.com, for PDF files to print.

Plan Worksheet

In advance of making a plan, it may help to think about, and write down, what things are most important to you, what you hope to gain from a nap plan, and what your specific goals are.

The things that are most frustrating or disruptive to us now are:

_____

_____

_____

_____

_____

_____

_____

_____

What we hope to achieve from a nap plan is:

_____

_____

_____

_____

_____

_____

_____

Our Nap Plan

We will begin our nap plan for _____
(name)

on _____
(date)

Goals for our Daily Schedule (Wake Up, Eat, Sleep)

Approximate time	Activity

Goals for Consistent Wake-Up Time and Regular Nap and Sleep Times

Morning wake-up time is approximately: _____

My child's naptimes will be: _____

_____

Bedtime (lights out) is: _____

Specific Solutions We Will Use for Our Situation:

From page: _____ *Section heading:* _____
Description of the idea and what we will do:

_____

_____

_____

_____

_____

_____

_____

_____

From page: _____ *Section heading:* _____
Description of the idea and what we will do:

_____

_____

_____

_____

_____

_____

From page: _____ *Section heading:* _____
Description of the idea and what we will do:

_____

_____

_____

_____

_____

_____

From page: _____ *Section heading:* _____
Description of the idea and what we will do:

_____

_____

_____

_____

_____

_____

From page: _____ *Section heading:* _____
Description of the idea and what we will do:

_____

_____

_____

_____

_____

_____

From page: _____ *Section heading:* _____
Description of the idea and what we will do:

_____

_____

_____

_____

_____

A Persistent, Consistent Nap Plan Brings Success

Changing your child's naptime patterns can be a complicated undertaking. There are so many different factors to consider that the solutions aren't always simple to identify or to apply. In addition, children grow and change along the way, and their sleep needs change, too. In order to see the most pleasant and long-lasting changes, you'll want to follow these steps:

• **Make a commitment to identify your child's sleep issues.** Every child is different, so it is impossible to create a one-size-fits-all nap solution. It takes detective work to clearly identify your child's sleep issues. The issues are also different for each parent, and your needs must be taken into consideration as well.

• **Find the right solutions.** Each family has its own philosophy about life. You cannot blindly accept someone else's prescribed solution and expect it to work for you. It's important to choose solutions that suit your family, your beliefs, your child, *and* your sleep needs.

• **Organize solutions into a complete plan.** Reading about good ideas is only the beginning. You must organize them into a plan. Writing them down will be most helpful, so that you can remember all the parts of your plan as you go through your day.

- **Follow your plan in total every day.** Making a grocery list but then going out for a walk in the park won't fill your refrigerator any more than making a nap plan and leaving it in the book will solve your sleep problems. Commit to following your plan, and positive changes are inevitable.
- **Be flexible enough to make adjustments as necessary.** It's not always possible to make a perfect plan from the get-go. Sometimes it takes a few adjustments as you work through the ideas. While you should give each idea enough time to settle, you should also be looking to make adjustments along the way until you feel that you've settled on your best solutions.
- **Be realistic enough to have reasonable expectations.** It takes time to experience change. Let's face it, no matter how good your plan is, there are times it will be impossible to follow—you'll be out at a birthday party past naptime, or your child will come down with a cold. Don't beat yourself up over these natural digressions. Just dust yourself off and start anew. If you stay the path, your child will be napping well in no time.
- **Keep your perspective.** It isn't always easy, but it is immensely helpful to keep your perspective and maintain a feeling of joy. Nap problems can take time to solve, but in the big picture of life, it is but a blink. Children are little for a very short time, and parents of older kids will tell you that these early years are the most magical of childhood. The things you'll remember most are the adorable little antics, the sweet smiles, and the joy-filled pleasures of raising a little one.

Part 2

Newborn Babies

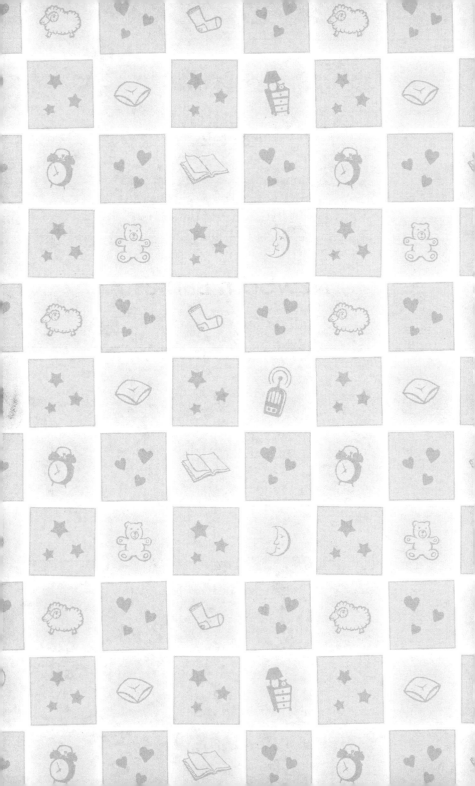

Growing into a
Napping Rhythm

The actions we take with our newborn babies set the stage for good napping habits later. Seemingly innocent caretaking patterns can develop into barriers to good napping. To prevent problems from cropping up, treat your newborn's daytime sleep hours as precursors to future nap behavior. It helps to understand how newborn napping rhythms develop and change so that you can take the actions that set your child up for years of great napping ahead.

The Nature of Newborn Sleep

Newborn babies sleep a lot, but here's the challenge: they don't actually *nap*. Their fifteen to eighteen hours of daily sleep are distributed evenly over four to seven brief periods—day and night. Premature or sick babies will likely sleep more overall hours, but they sleep for shorter spans, so they divide their sleep into six to ten sleep periods.

Since we adults don't break our own sleep into small chunks throughout the day and night, our new babies' sleep schedules can appear strange. We want our babies to conform to a "normal" pattern of sleep. But for your newborn, this haphazard pattern *is* normal. This pattern is the same as what your baby experienced while in the womb, and it feels right to him. What he is experiencing is *normal newborn sleep*.

The term *newborn* does not have an exact definition. When it comes to sleep, we'll use the term *newborn* to include babies up to four months old (for premature babies this is adjusted age—based

> ### Professional-Speak
>
> "Your baby's nine months—or three trimesters—is a time of unbelievably complex development. Nevertheless, it takes most babies *an additional* three months to "wake up" and become active partners in the relationship. This time between birth and the end of your baby's third month is what I call your baby's 'Fourth Trimester.'"
>
> **—Harvey Karp, M.D., author and creator of the book, CD, and DVD *The Happiest Baby on the Block***

on your due date). You are the best judge of your own baby, so let your instincts guide you to know when your baby graduates from the newborn stage into babyhood and a more structured day/night sleep pattern.

Sleep Consolidation: Growing from Newborn to Baby

Sleep consolidation is a biological process whereby your baby begins to sleep fewer overall hours while those hours consolidate so that the majority occur during nighttime, and daytime sleep settles into two or three longer naps. Sleep consolidation begins when your baby is two months of age or older. Biological consolidation is just the beginning, though—it doesn't automatically equal great naps and sleeping through the night. It just opens the door for a process that takes time to mature and many months to complete. What's more, individual development and temperament, plus cultural, social, and other outside factors, all have an influence on your baby's sleep patterns.

To understand your newborn's sleep pattern, it can help to consider that not too many days ago your baby was nestled in the sleep-inducing womb. The environment was consistent and perfect for sleep, and your baby slept twenty hours a day or more. Waking periods were random and for very short periods of time. The kicking and poking that you felt were often movements made during sleep—a fetus is a very active sleeper.

The moment after birth, your child doesn't drastically or instantly change—your newborn will continue the same sleep-wake pattern for weeks. At this time you will be adjusting to life as a new parent, which takes a tremendous amount of energy, and perhaps recovering from childbirth as well. (This, by the way, is the scientific justification for you to sleep when your newborn sleeps!)

During the newborn stage it is hard to separate the facts that pertain to naps versus those that apply to nighttime sleep, since they are so closely intertwined. Therefore, the benefit here is that when you understand how to help your newborn take better naps, you'll likely also see an improvement in her nighttime sleep.

Key Point

Pay attention to the nap routines that you are creating with your newborn baby. Construct patterns that you will be comfortable continuing for three or four months. Stay alert to signs that your baby's sleep biology is maturing, and make appropriate changes. If you miss the transition from *newborn* to *baby*, you may find that today's routines will continue for a year or longer.

Nap Facts
Newborn Babies

Newborns cannot be put on a sleep schedule, and it can be dangerous to your infant's well-being to even try. During the first weeks of your baby's life, he sleeps when he is tired—it's that simple. You may be able to force a new baby to sleep by manipulating his environment, and you can wake him up when he is sleeping soundly, but it's not an easy task. The best approach for your newborn is to respect his sleep needs. Learn how to read his sleepy signals and allow him to sleep when he wants to sleep.

Newborn Babies Have Short Sleep Cycles

Not only do newborns have very short sleep cycles, they wake easily between cycles. This pattern is thought to act as a protective device—babies need lots of care and feeding, and they need to gain the attention of others to tend to their needs. Infants require food every few hours, so their light sleep cycles accommodate their need to wake to eat. Babies who are born prematurely or with special needs will sleep even more lightly with shorter sleep cycles, which is nature stepping in to be sure these special babies get the extra care that they require.

New Babies Need to Eat Frequently

In the womb, babies don't need to think about eating. Because their nutritional needs are continuously met, they never feel hunger. After birth, babies must adjust to a different reality. Hunger is a new sensation. Furthermore, they are growing rapidly, their tummies are small (the size of one miniature fist), their diet is liquid, and it digests quickly. To fuel their amazing growth, newborns need to eat every two to four hours—and sometimes more frequently—day and night.

By the time your baby is three to four months old, he'll be able to "sleep through the night," which for an infant means five consecutive hours of sleep without waking for a feeding. (A small number of babies achieve this milestone sooner.) It's important to realize that even when your baby begins to sleep for seven or more hours at a stretch, he may begin that span at 7:00 P.M., which means he'll be waking for a feeding at 2:00 A.M.

Newborn Babies Do Not Need to Be "Taught" How to Sleep

New babies don't need sleep lessons. They've been sleeping for twenty hours a day in the womb—they *know* how to sleep! New-

Vivian and Hudson, twins, four days old

born babies don't have sleep problems, either. However, their environment can cause disruption to the sleep that they crave. If allowed to follow their own personal sleep patterns, infants will sleep as much as they need to, whenever they need to. It is a parent's job to protect their new baby's need for sleep and provide a safe and comfortable place for it to occur at the right times.

Babies don't fight sleep on principle, but they will fail to sleep if the routine doesn't match their needs. If you understand your baby's napping needs and put him down for naps at the right times, he will welcome them.

Newborns Like to Sleep on Their Tummies, but They Need to Sleep on Their Backs

Major pediatric groups recommend that almost all newborns sleep on their backs as the most effective method of reducing the risk of sudden infant death syndrome (SIDS). The occurrence of SIDS has decreased by over 50 percent since the recommendation was first made in the 1990s. Any exceptions should be approved by a medical professional, and other safeguards should be taken to protect the baby. (If your baby resists sleeping on his back, see the ideas beginning on page 185.)

Babies Are Noisy Sleepers

Most newborns are not calm, quiet sleepers. They grunt, coo, whimper, and even cry in their sleep. These are what I call *sleeping noises*, and your baby is sound asleep during these episodes.

Babies move through sleep cycles and shift from deep sleep to light sleep with brief awakenings between cycles. If your baby is not hungry, she may move around, make noises, get resettled, and fall back to sleep on her own. However, if a parent rushes to her side in the middle of this process, she will wake up fully. The result is a wide-awake but overtired baby! Over time, this process of being fully awake between cycles becomes a baby's adopted sleep pattern, preventing the natural elongation of sleep spans from occurring.

This experience is particularly common for breastfeeding, cosleeping mothers. They become very tuned in to their baby's every noise or movement—which is, of course, wonderful. The problem is that mothers often interpret every sound or action as a cue to put baby to the breast. My fourth baby, Coleton, would merely sniff and I would attach him—almost by instinct, in my sleep! The problem here is that half the time, the baby is making sleeping noises or merely "getting comfortable." My Coleton eventually learned how to put himself back to sleep on his own when I started allowing him to do so.

Newborn Babies Are Active Sleepers

During sleep, your baby's little fingers will twitch, his legs and arms will move, and his facial expressions will change. He may make sucking motions, and he will change his entire position, squirming or fidgeting. All of this activity is normal, and it is done during sleep, so it doesn't require any intervention from you.

Newborn Babies Cannot Be Spoiled

New babies cannot manipulate people, and they can't be stubborn. Their needs are basic instinct. They require pampering, and they deserve as much holding, cuddling, nursing, and rocking as we can give. As a matter of fact, studies tell us that babies who are carried and cuddled throughout the day will fuss and cry less than those left too often to their own devices.

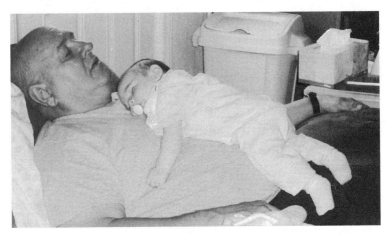

Granddaddy Gary and Evan, six months old

Parents of Newborns Need Time for Adjustment

This is a unique and wonderful time for you. It is time to learn about this brand-new little person in your life. Be open to letting your baby tell you about himself. Don't try to make him fit into any preconceived image that others have created for you about babies and sleep. Relax, enjoy, follow your baby's lead, and take things one day at a time.

Professional-Speak

"When it comes to sleeping, whatever your baby does is normal. If one thing has damaged parents' enjoyment of their babies, it's rigid expectations about how and when the baby should sleep."

—James McKenna, Ph.D., Director, Mother-Baby Behavioral
Sleep Laboratory, University of Notre Dame,
www.nd.edu/~jmckenn1/lab

Nap Tips for Newborns

Now that we've covered some basic information about newborn sleep, we'll move on to some tips for working with your baby's natural biology. By respecting and understanding his needs you can respond to him in ways that bring the best sleep for your baby, and for you, too.

Learn to Differentiate Between Sleeping Sounds and Awaking Sounds

When you put your newborn down for a nap and later hear noises, don't immediately run to pick her up. First, stop and listen for a few minutes, and then peek in on her without her seeing you. If you are co-sleeping with your baby and he begins to make noises, don't move—just listen. Cue in to your baby's sounds and movements to determine if he is awake, making sleeping noises, or shifting sleep cycles. Many babies have amazing radar and can tell when Mommy or Daddy is awake or hovering at the doorway, so use a baby monitor or stay out of sight until you know that your baby is really awake.

If your baby is awake and hungry, you'll want to feed her, of course. You don't want her to have to cry to get your attention. But if she's just being a noisy sleeper or moving through her sleep cycle, let her be, and let her sleep!

Watch for Signs of Tiredness

Possibly the most effective newborn tip is to get familiar with your baby's sleepy signals and put him down for a nap immediately

Mother-Speak

"I learned that I should never let my baby cry, so I went to her the minute she made a peep. I was so proud of my baby-soothing skills because half the time she would be back to sleep by the time I got to the rocking chair. But then I realized I was taking a sleeping baby from her cradle!

Now I give her ten minutes. If she doesn't settle down but still isn't outright crying, I use a broomstick to lean over and rock the cradle, and I turn on her white noise machine. Half the time she *does* go back to sleep. To think of all the extra sleep I could have had . . ."

—**Andrea, mother to three-month-old Isabella**

when he seems tired. A baby who is encouraged to stay awake when his body is craving sleep is an unhappy baby. Over time this pattern develops into sleep deprivation. A pattern of staying awake past sleepiness also complicates developing sleep maturity; it can disrupt your baby's ability to fall asleep easily, leading to a baby who requires a long, involved routine before every nap or nighttime sleep.

Learn to read your baby's sleepy signs and put him to bed as soon as that window of opportunity presents itself. Watch your baby for any of these common newborn sleepy signs:

- A lull in movement or activity; calm, slower movements
- Quieting down, making fewer or simpler sounds
- Losing interest in people and toys
- Appearing glazed or unfocused; staring off in the distance
- Fussing or whining
- Eyes open wide and unblinking
- Rubbing eyes or ears
- Yawning
- Being awake for one to three hours

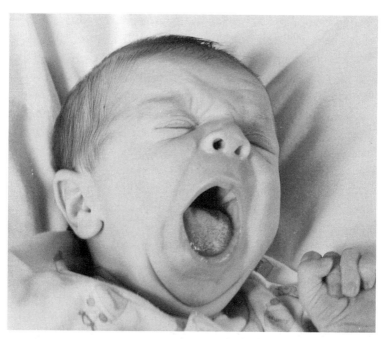

Gabriel, one month old

Here are a few signs that your baby might be overtired or very hungry:

- Fretful crying
- Arching backward or going rigid
- Flailing, jerky, uncoordinated movements of arms and legs
- Drooping eyelids, slow blinking, eyelids fluttering
- Dark circles appearing under the eyes; eyes appearing bloodshot
- Being awake for more than three hours

Determine If Your Baby Is *Hungry* or *Tired*

Babies might fuss, whine, or cry if they are *either* tired or hungry. So, how can you tell the difference? First, become familiar with your baby's usual tired signs from the previous list. Note your baby's behavior in the minutes before he either eats or falls asleep. Since every child is unique, you will notice your particular baby's ways of communicating that she is tired or hungry.

You can often tell if your baby is fussing because she's *hungry* if she is rooting (moving her head back and forth and opening her mouth), thrusting her tongue, sucking on her fingers or hands, increasing her level of activity, or fussing and doesn't stop when you pick her up. The clock can also help you make this distinction—if it has been two to four hours since your baby's last feeding (depending on your baby's typical pattern and whether she is breastfed or bottlefed), her fussing is likely a sign of hunger. According to the American Academy of Pediatrics, if your newborn is crying, that is a *late* indicator of hunger, so watching for these early hunger signs can prevent crying.

Use the Power of Daylight

A simple way to cue your baby toward a regular day/night sleep schedule is by taking advantage of the effect that daylight has on sleep patterns. There is a powerful structure wired into the human brain right from birth that interprets daylight as active and alert time. Within the first few months of life, your baby will take in these light cues to help consolidate sleep patterns.

The most effective light for signaling alert time is natural daylight. Make an effort to expose your baby to daylight first thing in the morning. You might provide your baby's first feeding near a window that lets in morning light. If it is dark outside, the second choice is artificial light. You can also play with your baby in bright daylight several times throughout the early part of the day, furthering the announcement that daytime is awake time. By doing this consistently, you can help your baby organize his day and night sleeping pattern.

Encourage Sleepiness with Darkness Cues

The second half of the biological sleep-cue equation is that darkness signals to the brain that it is time to sleep. Darkness encourages the release of the body's natural sleep hormone, melatonin. This is a very powerful natural phenomenon that allows your baby to be tired and fall asleep easily at bedtime.

Babies will tend toward an early bedtime, around 6:30 or 7:00 P.M., but since this is hours away from the parent's bedtime, the house can be lit up as bright as daytime. The bright light signals to your baby's brain that it is time to be alert and active. You can protect this natural melatonin-creation process by keeping the lights dimmed in the hour before your baby's bedtime.

A second aspect to this process involves keeping the darkness throughout the night. Even a small night-light can disrupt sleepiness and begin the alerting process—which you don't want happening at 2:00 in the morning! Keep night-lights small and away from your baby's face. Keep glowing clocks turned away from your baby's bed. Don't turn on bright lights or the television during midnight feedings. Darkness can keep your baby in a sleepy state, allowing him—and you—to fall back to sleep easily after diapering and feeding.

Keep Night Feedings Hushed, Mellow, and Toy-Free

As strong as the release of the melatonin hormone is, the process can be halted with enough action going on nearby, causing your baby to pull out of sleepiness and into alertness. A fun parent, an interesting toy, a familiar song—any of these can jar a baby out of his sleepy state. Once your baby has become alert, you'll have to guide him into the descent into tiredness all over again.

By keeping nighttime as quiet as possible, you encourage your baby to recognize these quiet, dark times as sleeping times. You'll also keep him in a semi-sleepy state, from which it is much easier to return to deep sleep.

Make Use of Soothing Sounds

The environment that your baby enjoyed in the womb was not a quiet one. There was a constant symphony of sound. (Remember those whooshing sounds from when you listened to your baby's heartbeat?) Because of this prenatal history, "white noise" sounds or soft music can help babies to relax and fall asleep—and stay asleep—more easily than a totally quiet room.

Another benefit of soothing sounds during naps is that they block out other noises that might wake your baby before he is ready to naturally awaken. Sounds like dishes clinking or siblings playing can be intrusive sounds that wake your sleeping newborn. Having white noise or music playing can mask any of these baby-waking noises. In addition, your baby will become accustomed to these sounds for falling asleep, so they become an easy-to-use sleep cue, at home or away.

The sounds that help a baby to fall asleep and stay asleep are those that are steady and repetitive, without any major changes in volume or pitch. For newborns, a great option is a CD recording of sounds from the womb. These sounds are familiar to your newborn and often are effective at helping a baby take a nice, long nap. Other wonderful options are noise machines or CDs that play various "white noise" options such as rainfall, a babbling brook, or ocean waves. Choose sounds that soothe your baby and that you will be happy to listen to as well. Once your baby is familiar with these as his sleep cue, they can be used effectively for years to come.

Some babies prefer actual music. If you opt for music for your baby, choose carefully. You'll want to find relaxing tunes, such as classical or soft jazz music. There are a wide variety of recordings available that have been created specifically for relaxation, yoga, meditation, or sleep that make great options for your baby.

Daddy Chad; Kami, two years old; and Jason, two months old

The level and type of noise that disrupts sleep is different for each baby. Some children can sleep through a fire alarm siren, but some are awakened by the slightest noise. No matter what kind of sleeper your baby is, white noise or soft music can be helpful in three aspects. First, the gentle, consistent sound can be very effective at soothing your baby to sleep. Second, it can filter out other noises that can jar her awake. Third, it creates a consistent cue; when your baby hears the sound, she knows it's time to sleep.

Swaddle Your Baby for Naps

Newborns arrive from the womb, where they felt a continuous, warm pressure on every part of their body. Now, lying in a crib with three-quarters of their body lacking that ever-present pressure, many newborns are unable to fall asleep or stay asleep for long. In addition, their reflexive startle movements can wake them as they are falling asleep, or between cycles of sleep. Many babies can be comforted when parents create a womblike setting

Professional-Speak

"Rocking a baby to sleep in the first few months of life is often not only necessary but hugely rewarding for parents and baby alike. For your baby, it might feel close to being in utero—wrapped in the warmth of your arms, close to your heartbeat, and moving with the rhythm of your body motions. There is a precious short time when this is the most helpful way to get your baby to sleep."

—Jean Kunhardt, M.A., author of *A Mother's Circle:*
An Intimate Dialogue on Becoming a Mother

for sleep by wrapping them securely in a receiving blanket or specialty swaddling blanket.

Not all babies want or need to be swaddled, so if your baby sleeps fine without this, don't feel you must try this idea. However, parents who have babies who are colicky, fussy, or sensitive sleepers may find swaddling to be a lifesaver. You can learn more about swaddling—when to, how to, and weaning—on page 192.

Provide Your Baby with Rhythmic Movement

In the womb your baby was jostled and rocked all day long. The fluid sway of movement was a soothing sleep inducer. Because of this experience, many newborns find lying on a still surface the least comfortable way to sleep. Over the first few months of life, most babies will adjust to a motionless sleeping surface, but some need a bit more time and help to make the transition.

The most obvious place for your baby to find this womblike feeling is in your arms or a baby sling or carrier, which can be a newborn's ideal happy sleep place. As long as you are comfortable

Father-Speak

"Our baby napped exclusively in her swing for months. I work at home, and I kept the swing next to my desk. It was the only way I could get Anna to sleep for more than twenty minutes. Eventually she grew too big for the swing and started sleeping in her crib in my office. If she woke mid-nap, I would jostle the crib, and she would return to sleep. Now the crib is in her room (with a radio set to a talk station), and she takes a two-hour nap. Honestly though, the swing was worth its weight in gold for me when she was an infant."

—Hector, father of eleven-month-old Anna

and willing, an in-arms nap is pure joy to your baby. I strongly recommend that you balance these in-arms naps, at least half the time, with out-of-arms naps. A large number of babies who spend their early weeks of life in arms are unwilling to give this up for a flat, hard bed. (Smart babies!)

There are a wide variety of other options for creating movement for your newborn's naps. Baby swings, cradles, baby hammocks, vibrating seats, and strollers all will provide the perfect type of movement for naptime. Experiment with which ones appeal most to you and your baby. To learn more about movement sleep choices and get information about when and how to wean from movement, see the solutions on page 166.

Consider Offering Your Baby a Pacifier for Sleep

Once breastfeeding is established, it is fine to offer your baby a pacifier to help him fall asleep. There is no evidence that using a pacifier creates any health or developmental problems for young

Professional-Speak

"If used sensibly and for a baby who has intense sucking needs—in addition to, not as a substitute for, human nurturing—pacifiers are an acceptable aid."

—**William Sears, M.D., author of** *The Baby Book*

babies. On the contrary, new studies show that pacifier use may actually reduce the risk of SIDS, although it is unclear why the connection exists. At this time, medical organizations no longer discourage the use of pacifiers for babies up to one year of age, so if your baby benefits from having a pacifier for sleep, you can now rest assured that it is fine to use one.

Scientists and breastfeeding groups feel that more research needs to be done before a blanket recommendation of pacifier use can be made since it might interfere with the quantity or length of breastfeeding, so watch the news and talk this over with your health care professional.

Balance Co-Sleeping with Independent Sleeping

If you co-sleep with your newborn at night, consider letting your newborn nap in his own cradle or crib. Since it will be unlikely that you'll want to take a nap every time your baby naps or go to bed at night as early as your baby should, it will be very helpful if he is comfortable sleeping on his own.

Many co-sleeping babies adjust to having a different sleep place for naps versus nighttime sleep. Often a motion nap is a good solution for a baby who prefers to sleep with company, since the motion provides some of the sensory stimulation your baby receives from sleeping with you.

The additional benefit to having your co-sleeping baby sleep in a cradle or crib at naptime is that when then time comes to wean him from your bed at night, he will already be accustomed to sleeping alone, which should make the transition easier.

Provide a Cozy Cradle

Many newborns feel overwhelmed in a large crib. Your baby may find that a smaller cradle, bassinet, or baby hammock is more to her liking. There are many options for newborn beds, and it can be useful to shop around. There are cradles made especially for use beside an adult bed, which is helpful for ease of night feeding and for reaching over to settle your baby. A cradle that rocks or sways is a good option since this often can help your new baby sleep better.

Create a Nest

Because newborns spent nine months free-floating while curled in the fetal position, many are uncomfortable lying flat on their backs on a firm mattress. However, back sleeping on a firm mattress is the most important protection against SIDS. If your newborn naps well only in a sling or in your arms, this aversion to flat, stiff positioning may be part of the issue.

An idea that helps many newborn babies take longer naps is to place them to sleep in an infant seat, swing, or stroller. Safety dictates that you keep your baby within eyesight if using this suggestion. Watch to be sure your baby doesn't slump over with his head down, as this can lead to breathing problems. Help keep your baby's head up by using car-seat padding created for this purpose.

As a safe option for your newborn's nest, check into a baby hammock. These gently embrace your baby and allow a similar free-floating, 3-D type of movement as felt in the womb. Hammocks have a slight angle, raising the head of the bed, and can be rocked either by the baby's movement or with your gentle nudge. Hammocks are especially soothing for a baby with reflux, colic, or extreme fussiness. They can be wonderful for a baby who resists back sleeping and helpful for preemies or babies with special needs. There are a variety of styles available, so shop around.

A potential drawback to this idea is that your baby may get used to sleeping in his nest and resist future attempts to have him sleep in his bed, but you'll have many months of nice, long naps before you'll have to address this possible issue. Once your baby has passed the newborn stage, you can begin to intersperse these "nest" naps with sleeping on a flat crib surface to help make the transition.

Give Your Baby Opportunities to Fall Asleep Unaided

Newborns are incredibly soft and sweet. It's easy to keep such a precious package in your arms or in a sling, even after they have fallen asleep. The hitch here is that your baby will easily become accustomed to being held as she falls asleep. She'll soon be *unable* to fall asleep on her own. She'll cry to protest the minute you place her in bed, as if to say, "Why am I here? Pick me up please so that I can sleep!"

You can avoid creating this almost inevitable scenario by placing your baby in her crib, cradle, hammock, or cradle-swing when she is comfortable and drowsy but not entirely asleep. It's perfectly fine to pat or rub her leg, head, or tummy as she drifts off. Just gradually make your touch slower and softer until your hand is lying still on her. Then slowly remove your touch.

There is no risk in *sometimes* holding your sleeping baby. I would never advise you to miss out on this unique and beautiful experience. But balance this with plenty of times when you put your baby in his bed when he is drowsy and relaxed but not asleep.

> **Mother-Speak**
>
> "I think one of the most helpful ideas was to put him down when he was tired but awake—he surprised me by allowing it so often!"
>
> **—Judith, mother of three-month-old Harry**

Be Thoughtful About Creating Patterns

While newborn babies don't have "habits," they don't stay newborns for long. Before you know it, your newborn becomes a baby who is accustomed to a specific routine. Babies get used to a certain pattern that becomes a very strong sleep cue, and then they are reluctant to accept change.

For example, if you rock your baby in the rocking chair before every nap, then that is the pattern that your baby comes to expect before naps. It becomes a very comfortable—and very strong—sleep cue. So, be thoughtful as you set up your baby's naptime routines.

Be Aware of Your Baby's "Suck-to-Sleep" Association

If you are breastfeeding your newborn, it's likely that she'll easily fall asleep during nursing, since over 80 percent of newborn nurslings do fall asleep breastfeeding. It's nearly impossible to prevent your baby from becoming drowsy as she nurses—it's a biological benefit of breastfeeding. However, there is something you can do to prevent creating a firmly ingrained habit of sucking to sleep that is very hard to change.

Here's the golden ticket: At least half the time, remove your baby from your breast when she is done feeding but before she begins the pacifying sucking that is nonnutritive but sleep-inducing. Before your baby is completely asleep, remove her from the breast and transfer her to bed to finish falling asleep there. You will likely need to pat, jiggle, or shush her to help her fall asleep, but having

Johari, four months old

her do this without the nipple in her mouth will show her that she can, indeed, fall asleep without this. The value of this idea is most clear among breastfeeding mothers who must nurse their *toddlers* fully to sleep for every nap and bedtime—so to avoid that scenario, start this idea today. (To modify an existing "suck-to-sleep" association, go to page 154.)

Don't Smoke Before Your Baby's Naptime

If you are a smoker, avoid lighting up in the hour before your baby's nap—especially if you breastfeed. According to Julie A. Mennella, a psychobiologist who completed an extensive study of breastfeeding mothers who smoke, "Infants spent less time sleeping overall and woke up from naps sooner when their mothers smoked prior to breastfeeding." Mennella's research demonstrated that nicotine levels peak in breast milk thirty to sixty minutes after smoking and are gone after three hours, so the more time you can place between smoking and your baby's prenap feeding, the better your baby will sleep.

Tune Out Other People's Bad Advice

Many people have very strong opinions about babies and sleep— even people who don't *have* babies have opinions! Much of this opinion and advice is inaccurate, misguided, or downright dangerous. Inoculate yourself against bad advice. Do your own research and know the facts so that you can minimize their effects on you.

As an example, some people will try to tell you that letting your baby cry it out will solve all your sleep problems. Not only is this dangerous advice when applied to a newborn, it is rarely a simple one-time solution. Even with older babies, crying it out must be done over and over again, often at the expense of baby's and parents' emotions.

Nap When Your Baby Naps

You've likely heard this advice already, and for very good reasons. New parents can find that taking care of a baby in addition to other responsibilities takes a toll on their mood, their health, and even their marriage. New mothers are more likely to suffer from the baby blues and postpartum depression if they don't take care of their own sleep needs. Taking your own daily nap can help you combat fatigue, and it can help you to be a better parent. Even a twenty-minute nap can rejuvenate you and help to offset your disturbed nighttime sleep, so definitely give it a try.

Create a Prenap Routine

Newborn babies don't require much of a bedtime routine, as they sleep and wake all through the day and night. However, after the first few months, your baby will find it easier to fall asleep if you help him "wind down" for twenty or thirty minutes before naptime. If you go from a bright, noisy room—playing with your baby with television noise in the background, for example—and

Professional-Speak

"New parents sometimes try to put their baby on what they view as a reasonable schedule. From the baby's point of view, that's not reasonable at all. The best solution is a compromise, letting the baby call the shots while providing a stable, predictable home environment. A baby given this freedom likely will eat and sleep better, and cry less than if you try to make the baby conform to your schedule from the start."

—**Michael Smolensky, Ph.D., and Lynne Lamberg,**
The Body Clock Guide to Better Health

then expect him to go directly to sleep, it's likely that he'll be too revved up to relax. In the time before a nap, avoid noisy situations, bright lights, and active stimulation. Create a short but peaceful prenap routine, including a quiet diaper change and soft sounds (such as lullabies), and perhaps a bit of baby massage. This will help your baby transition easily from awake to asleep and begin to build the cues that will be invaluable as your baby gets a bit older.

Relax and Be Flexible

It is a fact that your newborn *will* be waking you up at night and *will* be napping on an unpredictable, ever-changing schedule, so you may as well be flexible about sleep issues right now. Being frustrated about your newborn's sleep patterns won't change a thing. It won't help your baby's biology mature any faster, and it will distract you from your most important and wonderful job right now—getting to know your new baby and letting your new baby get to know you. Gradually, your newborn will consolidate her sleeping and begin to sleep longer spells during the night and combine short daytime sleeps into actual naps.

Part 3

Solving Napping Problems:
Customized Solutions for Your Family

WE HAVE ALREADY talked a great deal about how important naps are to your child's health, mood, and happiness, and consequently, to *your* health, mood, and happiness. So, it's likely that you are now a true believer in the magic of naps. But what if your child isn't a believer? What if your child won't nap when you want her to? Or what if naps are much too short or if your little one requires an elaborate ritual of parent acrobatics in order to sleep? That's when you get to be investigator, researcher, teacher, and the ultimate purveyor of all things nap!

The following section outlines the most common nap problems and provides a variety of solutions for each one. Scan through the topics for your child's nap issues and select those solutions that make the best sense for you and your child. Put together a plan using the guidelines in Part 1 of this book, or simply begin using the tips as soon as you read about them.

Nap problems can be complicated, and it may take a few adjustments to your plan along the way, but the end results are definitely worth every minute of effort.

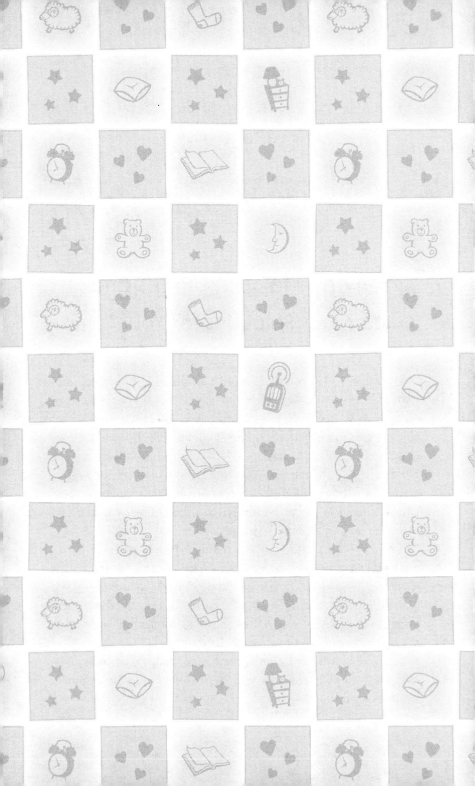

Catnaps
Making Short Naps Longer

....

See also: Newborn Babies (Part 2); Shifting Schedules:
Changing from Two Naps to One Nap; The Nap Resister:
When Your Child Needs a Nap but Won't Take One

> I have a four-month-old mini-napper! I can
> usually get her to go to sleep, but she always
> wakes up exactly forty minutes after I put her
> in bed. How can I get her to take longer naps?

This is an amazingly common occurrence. I have discovered that most mini-nappers are between two months and eight months old. Most of these babies fall asleep being fed or while in a car seat, sling, rocker, or someone's arms. They are then transferred to bed, where they sleep between thirty and fifty minutes. These factors clearly point to some possible causes and will lead us to the potential solutions.

Could It Be One-Cycle Sleep Syndrome (OCSS)?

In the first six to eight months of life, a baby's full sleep cycle ranges from forty to sixty minutes. When you add your baby's brief in-arms falling-asleep time together with the nap time, the total is *one sleep cycle*. If you'll recall from the first part of this book, human beings sleep in cycles, and there is a brief awakening between them. An independent sleeper will get comfortable and fall right back to sleep, likely not even realizing that he's awake. What this tells us is that a short napper cannot put himself back to sleep, so his nap appears to be over at the end of one sleep cycle. So, you see, it's likely that your mini-napper is suffering from what I call *one-cycle sleep syndrome* (OCSS).

Here's how to understand what's going on with your baby. Imagine this: It's your bedtime. You get into your nice, comfy bed with your favorite pillow and a soft blanket, and you fall asleep. If a while later you wake between sleep cycles and everything is exactly the same, you might change position, pull the covers up, and then fall right back to sleep, possibly without even remembering this happening.

What if you woke up to find yourself sleeping on the cold kitchen floor without blankets or pillow?

Would you simply turn over and go right back to sleep? I know I wouldn't! It's likely you would wake up shocked. You'd worry about how you got on the kitchen floor. You certainly wouldn't find it comfortable! In order to fall back to sleep you would have to go back to bed. Even though you would still be tired, you'd be wide awake by then. It may take time to get back to sleep. But you probably wouldn't sleep deeply because you would be concerned about ending up on the floor again.

This is how it is for a baby who is held, nursed, rocked, bottle-fed, or otherwise aided to sleep. She falls asleep under certain conditions, but at the end of her first sleep cycle, she wakes up briefly and finds herself in entirely different conditions. She startles, wondering, "What happened? Where am I? I can't sleep like *this*!" At this point she's awake, and you think naptime is over. But in reality, this is just the halfway point.

The key for many short nappers will be to identify the differences in conditions between *falling asleep* and *waking between cycles*. Then, you can either make these two conditions more similar or plan for the midcycle awakening and help your baby fall

Alyssa, one week old, and Aliyah, three years old

back to sleep when it happens. Lots of solutions and ideas will follow.

Nap Sleep Versus Night Sleep

Many babies who have OCSS for naps also have the same issue at night. While their sleep cycles may be longer or they might slide back into sleep between some of their cycles, they still require your assistance for many of their night wakings. Therefore, by identifying this problem and taking steps to solve it at naptime, you might also reduce or eliminate night waking.

Some babies, on the other hand, take short, one-cycle naps but sleep through the night just fine. How can that be? Actually, it is easy to understand. There are *many* conditions that occur for night sleep that are different from day naps. The house is darker and quieter at night. There are subtle routine changes, such as a bath and pajamas for bedtime but not at naptime. You act differently when putting your baby down for a nap versus when you put him down for nighttime sleep at the end of the day when you are tired and heading toward sleep yourself. In addition, all the biological forces at work on your baby's system function more compellingly at bedtime than they do during the day, such as homeostatic sleep pressure ("the Volcano Effect," page 14). Also, it's clear that your baby *will* eventually go to sleep at bedtime, even if it takes a while to settle him down, whereas naptime is often considered optional.

Do Children Who Sleep for Less than Thirty Minutes Have OCSS?

In order to be classified as OCSS, your baby would sleep more than a half hour. If your baby manages only a blink of a nap, then you're dealing with an entirely different problem. In five to thirty minutes, your baby will only be passing through stages 1 and 2 of sleep, which are the light sleep stages and from which he can easily be awakened.

If this describes your baby, you'll need to identify the conditions under which your baby gets *sleepy* and then how he falls *asleep* and what is happening in between to wake him up. For example, if he falls asleep in your arms but wakes up the minute you put him in bed, you can find solutions in the chapter "Changing from In-Arms Sleep to In-Bed Sleep" (page 136). If your baby is a great car-seat sleeper but can't be moved out of his seat, check page 198; if your baby breastfeeds or bottlefeeds to sleep, check page 154; and if your baby sleeps in a swing or vibrating seat, then check for solutions on page 166.

The Newborn Babies Exception

If your baby is newborn, she'll have an irregular sleep pattern for the first four to eight weeks, and catnaps are common. You will enjoy your new baby more if you stop wishing for two-hour naps and instead take cues from your newborn. It's time to go with the flow and be patient. Also, your newborn can stay awake for only one to three hours before needing another nap, and catnappers will often be closer to the one- to two-hour range.

You'll see a more regular pattern emerge over time. By learning the facts in Part 2, "Newborn Babies," and casually following the tips in this section, you can give nature a bit of a nudge toward regular, longer naps.

Newborn baby catnappers can often be coaxed into long, blissful naps by being carried in a sling carrier. If you are comfortable wearing your newborn for naps, then allow him to have some naps in a sling, maybe one each day, perhaps at his fussiest period of the day. Newborn sling-naps are a beautiful life experience for both of you. Be cautious, though, that you don't sling your baby for every nap, because then you'll likely be facing a difficult transition to naps in his bed when he gets a little bit older.

Is OCSS Always a Problem?

A one-cycle nap is not *always* a problem that requires attention. There are some babies who sleep for one cycle and cannot be coaxed into a longer nap no matter what solution you attempt. There are a small percentage of children who seem to be perfectly suited to a catnapping schedule. You will be able to tell if your child is a natural catnapper if after a short nap, he

- usually wakes up happy, refreshed, and alert
- stays cheerful until the next sleep period, whether it's the next nap or bedtime

- goes to sleep easily at naptime
- sleeps an overall adequate number of sleep hours (See chart on page 8.)

It is likely that a child who meets these conditions will be perfectly served by his short nap schedule. If your child is happy and well rested with his catnapping routine, then the biggest issue is for you to learn how to schedule your days around your little catnapper. The best resolution for you may be to figure out how to do most anything with your little company as part of the process. Save those tasks that you cannot do with your baby for those short naptimes, and get right to it as soon as his head hits the pillow.

If you determine that your child is a perfect catnapper, don't assume that it will always be that way. It is possible the he will eventually take longer naps as his sleep cycle lengthens.

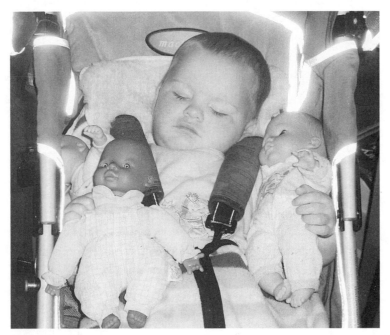

Analiese, fifteen months old

A contented catnapping baby is rare. Most children do not fall into the happy-with-a-short-nap category. For all those babies, we'll now talk about what causes OCSS and various solutions to help your baby take a longer nap.

Solutions for Gaining Longer Naps

While I suspect that most short nappers have one-cycle sleep syndrome, it doesn't mean that there is only one *solution* to gaining longer naps. Just like any parenting problem, there are as many solutions as there are children who need them! The remainder of this chapter is a menu of various solutions. Choose as many as suit you and experiment with them. Modify your plan as you go, and scan the rest of this book for additional ideas to add to your plan. Don't be afraid to modify what you learn based on your child's needs, since you know your child better than anyone else.

Create a Cycle-Blender Nap

One way to help your baby sleep through from one cycle to the next without waking is to put him down for a nap in a setting that will lull him back to sleep when he has a brief awakening. The most common and effective "cycle-blender" naps occur in cradle-swings, rocking cradles, or baby hammocks. Any of these options can help catnappers extend their sleep time because when your

---

Mother-Speak

"Our baby took only forty-minute naps in her crib. She takes two-hour naps in her cradle-swing—it has been pure sandman magic."

—Fiona, mother of four-month-old Jaelyn

baby begins to awaken, the rhythmic motion can help lull him back to sleep. (For more information about motion naps, see page 166.)

If you don't wish to purchase a swing just for napping, you can create a wonderful "cycle-blender" nap for your baby in his stroller. If it fits your schedule and lifestyle, a daily walk outside is good for both of you. If you prefer, you can bring your stroller in the house. (Or use inside and outside walks in combination.) Inside, walk your baby around the house until he falls asleep. You can even just roll the stroller back and forth over a ridge like a doorway threshold, as this is often relaxing for a baby. When your baby falls asleep, park the stroller near you. If he starts to move about or make noises, resume walking or give him a bit of a bounce and jiggle.

Once your baby gets used to taking a longer nap in the stroller, then you can begin to make a step-by-step transition to naps in the bed. Start by reducing the amount and intensity of movement, rolling slower and for less time. After your baby is asleep, park the stroller in a quiet place, perhaps in baby's own bedroom, next to his crib, to help him get familiar with that sleeping place. Listen in with a baby monitor, and if he makes noise mid-nap, try the jiggle and roll to see if your baby will return to sleep. Over time, work toward letting him fall asleep in the stationary stroller. If your baby is a deep sleeper who can be moved when he's sleeping, move him to bed when he's asleep to help him get used to taking naps in his crib.

To further enhance the "blend" and add to the nap-inducing ambience, keep the environment dark. To help soothe your child through sleep-cycle changes, add white noise, a recording of nature sounds, or soft, relaxing music to your routine. This can also mask noises from elsewhere in the house that can wake a child who is just shifting through to the second sleep cycle. Improving the quality of the air may help as well, particularly for a baby with asthma, allergies, or reflux, so consider using a humidifier or air purifier in your baby's room.

Set up the napping room and the sounds in advance so that everything is ready before your baby falls asleep and is kept on throughout the entire nap.

Build a Better Bed

Many catnappers will fall asleep at first because they are so tired that they welcome sleep. Then, after a short nap, the edge has been taken off, and a brief awakening turns into a full awakening. If you want to entice your baby to have a long nap, re-create the crib environment into a cozier nest. If the bed is comfortable, your baby might fall back to sleep on his own. There is a full list of ideas on how to make the crib cozy on page 140.

Do a Comfort Check

Make sure that the napping environment is perfect for your child. What's right for one isn't for another, so this may take a bit of detective work. Think about the room temperature: too hot or too cold? Does your baby sleep better with the window open or closed? Is it too light or too dark? Is his sleeping attire comfortable and nonbinding? Does he sleep better with socks on or off? Would pajamas improve his nap? Are his diapers adequate for the job, or is cold wetness waking him?

Are You Correctly Interpreting Signs of Tiredness?

If you put your child down for a nap *before* he is tired or when he is *overtired*, he won't sleep as well as when you hit that perfect just-tired moment. Review the signs of tiredness on pages 44 and 88 and observe your child for these indicators. Put your child down for a nap the moment you see any indication of fatigue. If you take note of the time that this occurs over a period of a week or so, you should see a pattern emerge. This can help you set up a daily nap schedule that suits your child's tired times perfectly.

In addition to signs of tiredness, also watch to see how long your child has been awake. Remember from Part 1 that homeostatic pressure builds and children can stay awake for only a certain period of time until they receive a biological pull toward a nap. Take a peek at the sleep chart on page 8 for appropriate time spans between sleep periods.

Keep in mind that children grow and change, and their nap schedule should change with them. What's perfect today may be different from what is perfect next month or on any given day if it's particularly busy. Keep your eye on your baby *and* on the clock.

Intervene *Before* the Cycle-Change Awakening

Baby sleep cycles fall in a range of forty to sixty minutes, but because they spend varied amounts of time in each stage, there is not an exact time span—each baby is unique. Many babies will sleep for a precise amount of time before waking; others will be more affected by the activity of any certain day but will usually have a consistent pattern. So, the first step is to determine your baby's nap sleep cycle.

For a few days, pay close attention to your baby's naps. As you are preparing him for sleep, watch him and jot down the time when he closes his eyes and appears to be falling asleep. Put him in bed as you usually do, and then note the time that he wakes up. Calculate how long your baby sleeps before he wakes up. Time his naps for three or four days to find the exact length of his sleep cycle. If you can't identify a pattern, use the shortest time span you counted.

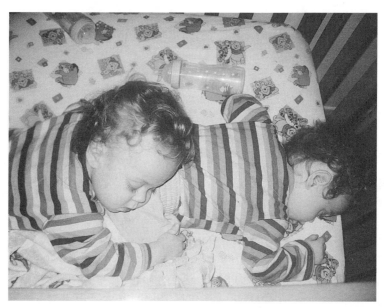

Alexander and Nicholas, twins, fourteen months old

Once you determine how long your baby typically sleeps, you'll be ready to intervene. Put your baby down for his nap as usual. About five to ten minutes *before* the usual wake-up time, go into the room and gently touch, pat, or jiggle your baby for about ten minutes. A good technique to try is to place your hands on the mattress near your baby and rhythmically pat or bounce the mattress. The jiggle and the patting sound can keep your baby sleeping. Another technique is to sit beside the bed and lay your hands on him. If your baby stirs, you can pat, rub, or shush him to prevent him from fully waking.

When you attempt this resettling procedure, your baby may slightly wake and then settle back to sleep for another cycle. Some babies may need you to reproduce the original setting under which they first fell asleep (nursing, rocking, pacifier). That might mean taking your baby out of bed and helping him fall back to sleep. Over time, you may be able to help your little one modify his body clock into taking longer naps. Once his system gets accustomed to this routine, you should no longer have to help him fall back to sleep between cycles.

Intervene at the Moment of the Cycle-Change Awakening

If your baby's naps are not consistent—they last thirty minutes, forty-five minutes, or an hour, but you never can tell which to expect—then your approach will have to be slightly different from the one just described. You'll need to wait until your baby actually stirs. This alternate method can also be used by your choice, if you would prefer to wait until your baby stirs rather than basing your response on timing. Instead of waking your baby *before* the cycle change, you'll intervene at the moment of awakening, when your baby moves or make noises that indicate he is shifting cycles.

To intervene at the moment of the sleep cycle change, you'll put your baby down for a nap as usual, but about fifteen minutes before the earliest possible awakening time, sit outside the bedroom and listen very carefully. (You can read a book, knit, or fold laundry—but be very quiet.) The exact minute that your baby makes a sound, go in to him quickly. You'll find him in a sleepy, just-about-to-wake-up state. Use whatever technique helps him to fall back to sleep—patting, breastfeeding, rocking, or offering a pacifier. If this doesn't work, you might even have to transfer him to a swing or vibrating seat. If you've caught him quickly enough, he will fall back to sleep. If you need to pick your baby up in order to resettle him and then want to return him to his bed, review the process for transferring your baby from arms to bed without waking him up (see "The Pantley Dance," on page 144).

If your baby doesn't go back to sleep but seems fussy and out of sorts, it's likely that you intervened too late and missed the window to get him back to sleep. Some babies wake quietly, and by the time they make a noise, they have already been up for a

Mother-Speak

"Your advice to sit outside the door and catch Kaiden the minute that he moves has worked wonders! The minute he stirs, I run in, put in the pacifier, and either pat him or pick him up and cradle him the exact same way I do to put him to sleep. Within ten minutes he is usually back into a deep sleep, and then he sleeps for another hour or more."

—**Noelia, mother of three-month-old Kaiden**

few minutes. In this case, you'll need to put your chair beside your baby's bed and watch him for signs of waking so you can begin your resettling attempts as soon as he begins to stir.

After a week or more of this intervention, your catnapper should be taking a much longer snooze without any help from you. However, even if your baby continues to need your help mid-nap to fall back to sleep, most parents are willing to make this effort to ensure that their baby gets a nice, long, refreshing nap every day.

Help Your Baby Discover How to Fall Asleep Without Your Help

Many catnappers wake fully between cycles because they absolutely, totally rely on you to help them fall asleep. If your baby *always* falls asleep with your help, such as breastfeeding, bottle-feeding, or being rocked, he may be physically unable to fall asleep any other way. In this case, it can help to very slowly wean your baby from your help over a period of several weeks. At the same time that you wean your baby from the sleep association that is getting in the way of him sleeping alone, you can build sleep cues such as darkening the room, putting your baby into bed with a small, safe lovey that he can cuddle with, and playing lullabies, nature sounds, or white noise.

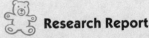
Research Report

Exposure to cigarette smoke can shorten your baby's naps, so it's best to prevent anyone from smoking in the same room or car as your baby. If you smoke cigarettes and breastfeed, avoid smoking for a minimum of one hour before your baby's naptime, and longer if possible, as it takes up to three hours to clear the nicotine from your milk.

As an example, if your baby relies on having you rock him until he falls asleep, then you would gradually reduce the intensity and amount of time that you rock him until you are holding him motionless in your arms. If you normally rock him in the family room, relocate your routine to the bedroom, moving right next to the crib. This will help your baby get used to the new location. The next step would be to place him in the crib while he is sleepy but still awake and keep your hands on him until he settles to sleep.

If your baby breastfeeds or bottlefeeds to sleep, the sucking-to-sleep routine is the strongest, most challenging association to change. See the chapter "Naptime Nursling: Falling Asleep Without the Breast, Bottle, or Pacifier," where you'll find many solutions for longer, easier naps.

If your baby is younger than six months, it may be very helpful to swaddle him for naptime (see the chapter "How to Use Swaddling for Naptime"). Putting your baby in socks can be helpful, too, to prevent cold feet from waking your baby prematurely.

Watch the Effects of Food, Drink, and Medicine

Catnappers can wake as a result of food and drink consumed prior to naptime. High-sugar, nonnutritious foods and beverages or foods that contain caffeine (such as chocolate) can disrupt sleep. Be sure that your child has a healthy, low-sugar snack before naptime.

Some medications may cause side effects such as sleeplessness or difficulty falling asleep, so if your child is taking regular medication, ask your health care provider about any potential influence it may have on your child's sleep.

Breastfeeding mothers who consume drinks that contain caffeine may find that this reduces the length of their baby's naps. Every baby has a different tolerance to the amount of caffeine in breast milk. Experiment with the amount and timing of consuming these beverages to see if they have an effect on your baby's naptime. You'll need to reduce the amount of caffeine in your diet for about two to three weeks to properly gauge the results of the change. (It may help to switch to drinks with less caffeine, such as tea or root beer, to prevent headaches that can result from a sudden elimination of caffeine.)

Have Realistic Expectations

As you work toward lengthening your child's naps, make sure that your goals are realistic and age-appropriate. For example, if your baby has a good night's sleep followed by two great naps, it's possible that his third nap of the day is perfect as a catnap. Your baby's naps should be based on a blending of science, biology, his daily needs, your needs, and your baby's sleep maturity and personality.

Settle and Wait

Just a quick note here that some babies are very capable of putting themselves back to sleep between cycles but no one ever gives them a chance to do this! Many babies are very noisy, active cycle-changers. Between sleep cycles, they shift around in the bed and make lots of noises. They may even make *slight* crying sounds. If no one shows up to get them, they will fall back to sleep. To test if your baby is able to do this, take a little longer getting to your baby once he wakes up—maybe allowing him ten or fifteen minutes to resettle. As long as he's not crying, just wait and see if he really is awake or if he is just noisily working his way through a sleep-cycle change. Some babies are not like this, and they quickly work themselves up to a wide-awake frenzy, so just try this once or twice to determine if your baby is a candidate for this solution.

Is It Time for a Schedule Change?

There are times when short naps are a sign that your baby's current nap schedule is no longer working for him and he is ready for a change of schedule—perhaps switching from four naps a day to three, from three to two, or from two to one. Possibly he needs more or less time between naps. Maybe he needs to go down for a nap a little earlier or later than he has been. Take another look at the sleep chart on page 8 and read the chapters "Shifting Schedules: Changing from Two Naps to One Nap" and "Shifting Schedules: Time to Give Up Naps?" which address schedule changes.

The "Heck with the Schedule, Just Watch the Baby" Approach to Naps

There are some families who would do best if they tossed aside any scientific sleep advice and lived completely according to baby's own pattern. If your lifestyle allows it and if it feels comfortable to you, then just ignore any charts, schedules, and advice, and let your child's signs of tiredness entirely dictate when he sleeps and how long he sleeps.

The key to this approach is to learn to read your child's signs accurately (see the list of signs on pages 44 and 88). Also, you

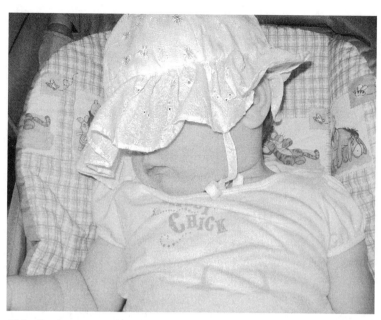

Abigail, eleven months old

must be willing to modify your daily activities according to your baby's sleep needs. This may mean holding your baby in a sling or a stroller for napping if you are out and about, or dealing with a fussy baby if he suddenly feels tired. It may be changing plans because suddenly your baby is tired and ready to sleep.

One aspect of this approach is that your baby's bedtimes will likely change from day to day depending on when and how long he napped. And, of course, if bedtime changes, then morning wake-up time will likely change as well. Therefore, this go-with-the-flow approach is best for families who are flexible in regard to bedtime and wake-up time.

There is nothing wrong with approaching your baby's sleep needs in this way. In order to be effective, though, it does require that you have a relaxed attitude about your child's sleep, coupled with plenty of knowledge and awareness, to be sure that his sporadic sleep schedule is meeting his true sleep needs.

Key Point

Health issues can interfere with your baby's sleep. Allergies, asthma, reflux, ear infections, colic, difficult teething, or a sleep disorder can affect your child's ability to take long, peaceful naps. If you suspect that your baby might be suffering from any of these ailments, talk to your pediatrician or other medical professional for advice.

Solve Nighttime Sleep Issues

There is a definite correlation between nighttime sleep and daytime naps in terms of length and quality. Many children who are not getting adequate nighttime sleep will often wake up early and then, an hour or so later, appear to need a nap but not nap long or well. So if you can improve your child's night sleep, he may well take better naps. If you are struggling with nighttime sleep issues, check my website, www.nocrysleepsolution.com, for excerpts from my No-Cry Sleep Solution books that address nighttime sleep problems.

The Nap Resister

When Your Child Needs a Nap but Won't Take One

....

See also: Shifting Schedules: Time to Give Up Naps?

> My daughter refuses to nap. If I put her in
> her crib, she will not sleep for love or money.
> She just cries until I rescue her, and then
> she's crabby for the rest of the day!

There are many reasons why children won't nap, and we'll delve into those in detail in a moment. Once you figure out the cause of your child's "nonnappingness," you can put together a plan to overcome her resistance. However, no matter why your child won't nap, there are a few tips that can be helpful as you encourage any child to nap. So keep these basic principles in mind:

- Maintain a consistent daily schedule that works with your child's natural body clock. Create a predictable pattern to the day.
- Modify your schedule according to your child's sleepy signs. (See pages 44 and 88.)
- Have a relaxing prenap routine to cue your child that naptime is here and to help him wind down and relax.
- Set up a sleeping place that is cozy and that sets the stage for sleep.
- Dress your child comfortably for sleep.

- Keep mornings bright and active and the half hour or so before each nap quiet and calm.

Answer the Question "Why Not?" and Then Look for Answers

There are many ideas for helping a child to nap, but the best idea in the world may not work for you if the solution doesn't address the reason that *your child* won't nap. Before you decide on a solution, you need to understand your child's motivation. Sometimes, just exploring the question "Why not?" is enough to get you started on the right path to your own best solution.

By identifying your child's specific causes, you can go on to creating a custom solution that will work best for you. So let's exam-

Arran, two years old

ine the typical reasons that children won't nap and see if you can identify the root of your child's reason or *reasons*, since there may be more than one that contributes to your child's resistance to napping. I'll identify the common reasons for nonnapping and then provide a few possible solutions for each issue. You'll likely have to combine two, three, or even four of these solutions with ideas from other parts of this book to come up with the perfect ideas for your little one.

Problem: Has Outgrown the Current Nap Schedule

During the first six years of life, children go through many changes in their napping patterns. They transition from many sporadic naps to three specific naps, then two, and finally one nap. And to make things more complicated, a child may go from two naps down to one and then back up to two naps again! If you try to have your child nap on an "expired" nap schedule, then he'll likely be unable to sleep when you ask him to.

Solutions

Think about how long you've been following the same nap schedule and if you need to make a change. Here are a few tips on figuring out if the schedule needs adjustment:

- Has your child evolved physically—for example, has he learned to crawl, pull up to a stand, or walk? Physical changes can signal a needed change in nap schedule.
- Has her feeding or meal schedule changed? The timing and amount of food can affect sleep times.
- Is she still waking up at the same time every morning? If her wake-up time has changed, it's likely her nap times will change too.

- Has there been a change in her daily routine—day care, playgroup, or a change in your schedule—that affects her ability to fall asleep at certain times?
- Is your child in a good mood upon awakening from a nap? Does her mood change between naps? Is she ready to sleep sooner than usual? Or later?

Professional-Speak

"Be forewarned: you may go through a period when your baby is totally miserable while you're trying to tweak his nap routine. Savor any signs of progress on the nap front rather than holding out for naptime perfection. After all, every baby step taken en route to naptime nirvana, however slowly or reluctantly, is a very big deal indeed."

—Ann Douglas, author of *Sleep Solutions for Your Baby,*
Toddler and Preschooler

Once you ponder the answer to the previous questions, set a plan. Use the sleep hours chart on page 8 as a guide to setting up a possible schedule. Take a peek at the sample schedules on pages 111 and 132. Sketch out what you think is a good plan and then use your child's daily signs of fatigue as indicators to when he should be napping. Adjust the plan over the next few weeks until you settle on the right schedule. It can take weeks for a child's biological clock to adapt to a new routine, so be patient during the transition.

Read over the chapters "Shifting Schedules: Changing from Two Naps to One Nap" and "Shifting Schedules: Time to Give Up Naps?" Once you've landed on a perfect routine you'll likely settle there for a while. But keep your eyes and ears open, as this will change again and again over the next few years.

Problem: Naptime Isn't Properly Aligned with Homeostatic Pressure

Remember the Volcano Effect described in Part 1 (page 14)? It explains how children have a natural time span that occurs between waking up and the need to return to sleep. When you put a child to bed *before* the span has passed, she won't easily fall asleep, but if you wait too long and miss her natural span, she'll have moved into a second wind and you'll have to work extra hard to help her regain her feeling of tiredness or wait until she hits another lull before attempting a nap.

Solutions

Seek the optimal length of time from awakening to naptime. To do this, jot down when your child wakes up (in the morning or after a nap), then use the chart on page 8 to figure out how many hours your child should be awake until the next nap. Beginning a half hour or so *before* the estimated time, watch your child for sleepy signs (pages 44 and 88). When you notice that he is looking tired, get him right off for a nap! Once you've settled on the best nap time, you can build a slightly longer prenapping ritual into your day. The ritual will help to fortify the new nap schedule.

Problem: Nap Schedule Doesn't Match Your Child's Biological Clock

Human beings naturally have times when they are feeling alert and times when they are tired, and this applies to babies and young children just as much as it does to adults. These alert or tired times can be affected by timing of meals, morning wake-up, bedtime, exposure to light and darkness, the activity of the day, and of course, the homeostatic sleep pressure that we've already covered.

Solutions

Take note of your child's energy level and mood throughout the day. See if you can identify the ups and downs of his biological cycle.

At the peak of your child's cycle he'll be energetic and active. This is often a time when we say, "This child needs a nap!" What that really means, though, is that you *missed* his low-energy phase when he was mellow and would have likely welcomed sleep, and now he's launched into his second wind—a difficult time to impose a nap. Instead, use this observation to set up for tomorrow's schedule, since children's tired spans occur at generally the same time each day. Monitor the awake time spans based on the sleep chart. These factors together can guide you to the best time for your child's nap, since a tired child will welcome sleep more than an alert, energetic child.

Problem: Nap Schedule Isn't Consistent from Day to Day

If your child's nap schedule varies from day to day, then his body clock will struggle to stay in sync with his naptime. For example, if on weekdays his naptimes, bedtime, and wake-up time are specific but on weekends they're hit and miss, then your child will be functioning with a weekly bout of jet lag. Other inconsistencies can also affect this, such as when your child naps at a certain time at day care but a different time at home, or if he takes a nice long nap on days when you are at home but takes a short one in the car (or skips a nap entirely) when you are on the go.

Solutions

Using the guidelines from the previous two sections, set up a possible nap schedule for your child, and do your best to stay within a

Ryan, eighteen months old

half hour of the naptimes that you have set up. Try to run errands or set playdates for times before or after naps. You won't forever be bound by these times, as children's sleep needs do change. But if your child gets cranky when she misses a nap, it's worth it to work your days around the nap schedule. When your child is sleeping on a regular schedule, then you'll find that missing a nap once or twice a week will be much easier for him to handle.

Problem: Overtired or Overwired by Naptime

Some children have subtle sleepy signs, and by the time they yawn and fuss, they are already overtired. Some children give off unique signs of fatigue that can be easily misinterpreted. Other times, parents are too busy to spot the signs. No matter the reason, if you miss your child's signs of fatigue, he can quickly move past his tired spell and into a second wind—that state of artificial energy that often brings with it more crying, fussing, whining, and tantrums. When you miss your child's tired signs, it also means he won't be able to fall asleep when you do put him in bed later.

Solutions

To learn your child's sleepy signs, it can help to watch him in the hour after he first wakes up in the morning, when he is well rested. Compare this to his behavior during the time from dinner to bedtime, when most children show signs of fatigue. As his usual bedtime draws near, make note of how his behavior and body language differs from when he is alert and refreshed.

While children are unique in their combination of signs of fatigue, your child may demonstrate one or more of these signs that tell you he is tired and ready to sleep:

- Reducing his level of activity; becoming more quiet
- Losing interest in playtime, people, or toys
- Rubbing his eyes, ears, or hair
- Looking glazed or unfocused; staring off into space
- Having a more relaxed jaw, chin, and mouth (droopy looking)
- Eyelids at half-mast, slow-motion blinks, or eyes open wide and unblinking
- Becoming whiny, cranky, or clingy
- Fussing, crying, or having tantrums
- Losing patience with toys or activities
- A burst of uncoordinated activity or hyperactive behavior
- Yawning
- Lying down or slumping in his seat
- Watching television or a movie with a blank expression
- Caressing a lovey or blanket
- Asking for or rooting for the breast, a pacifier, or a bottle

Father-Speak

"We've started watching Sam for sleepy signs and learned something important. In the past when he started to lose interest in toys, we would try harder to get his attention—getting louder and more energetic. He'd end up with a meltdown, and then it would take a half hour of rocking to get him to fall asleep. Now we realize that he's pulling away because he's tired. So we put him in the hammock and he goes right off to sleep."

—Hugh, father of six-month-old Samuel

Problem: Not Tired

It seems like a ridiculously obvious reason, yet it's easy to misinterpret or totally miss a child's signs of fatigue. A large number of parents struggle with little ones who won't nap, not realizing that their child simply is not at all tired when he is put in bed.

Solutions

If your child is wide awake and alert when naptime rolls around, don't rush him off to bed. Think of the irony of this situation: your child isn't feeling tired at all, but you think it's naptime so you try to force him into it. "Relax! Now!" you say. It's likely that the harder you try, the more awake he will become. It may be better to abort the trip to bed and take fifteen to thirty minutes to help him transition from the activity of the day to the relaxed state needed for sleep. Lower the lights or turn them off. Turn off the television and turn on soft music or white noise. Get him involved in a quiet activity such as reading, looking out the window, sitting on a rocker, or cuddling on the sofa. When your child begins to relax, then you can head to bed for a nap.

Another way to help an active child slow down to allow tiredness to set in is to use a relaxation technique such as massage or yoga. These practices hold many benefits, including relieving stress, improving sleep patterns, and enhancing the parent-child relationship.

If, despite your efforts, your child doesn't relax but gets more revved up, then look at the quiet time together as a bit of bonding and recharging and try for a nap later.

Problem: Hungry, Thirsty, or Overfull

It's not easy for a child to fall asleep if his tummy is rumbling from hunger or groaning from too much food. His sleep can also be disturbed if the wrong foods are eaten prior to sleeping time.

Solutions

Many foods can affect energy level and sleepiness. Some induce a feeling of calm and even drowsiness, some can create feelings of alertness, and others are neutral. This is due to certain chemicals contained in food and certain biological responses to foods that affect brain function.

Foods that energize or disrupt sleep can be avoided in the hour before naptime. A few examples of the foods to avoid prenaptime are red meat, bacon, sausage, caffeinated or carbonated beverages, chocolate, peppermint, citrus juice, butter, sugar, simple carbohydrates (such as white bread), and foods that are fatty, greasy, or spicy.

Conversely, foods high in whole-grain carbohydrates are known to have a calming, relaxing effect on the body. Other foods that are known to help create a calming effect are green, leafy vegetables and sunflower seeds. In addition, some foods contain tryptophan, a sleep-inducing chemical. Avoid sleep aids containing tryptophan or melatonin, as these can be dangerous when given to children. Stick to these real foods: turkey, tuna, or natural peanut butter without sugar. (Spread a small amount of peanut butter on bread, crackers, or fruit. Peanut butter alone can pose a choking hazard.) Other good prenap choices are milk, cottage cheese, hard cheese, yogurt, bananas, avocadoes, soy milk, tofu, soybeans, eggs, and of course the ultimate sleep-inducing food, breast milk.

Be cautious about having a child drink a great amount of fluids right before his nap (breast milk excluded). A soggy diaper or an urgent need to use the potty can disturb a child's sleep and cut a nap short.

Problem: New Milestones Are Preventing Sleep

A child who is new to a major development skill, such as rolling over, crawling, pulling to a stand, walking, learning to build a block tower, learning how to use a computer, or beginning potty training, can become so single-minded that he almost *can't* stop what he's doing to relax enough to fall asleep. Children have different temperaments; some can work on their skills during waking hours and put them aside during naps and bedtime, whereas others find it hard to shut off their physical practice.

Solutions

If your child is learning something new and exciting, make sure he has plenty of time to practice during the day. Then resort back to a familiar and routine activity in the half hour or so before nap to create a buffer between practice time and sleep time. (If standing in the crib is the issue, see page 217 for specific ideas.)

Problem: Reliance on a Sleep Association

A child who is accustomed to falling asleep in one specific way can become so used to this method that if you try to have him nap under any other condition, he would be physically unable to do so. Examine this from your own viewpoint. It's possible that you sleep well in your own bed but struggle to sleep on an airplane, at a hotel, or at someone else's home. Some children's sleep associations are so strong it can only be compared to asking you to sleep on a roller coaster when you are used to sleeping in your bed.

Solutions

The most common nap-preventing associations are breastfeeding or bottlefeeding to sleep, being held in loving arms, or sleeping in a swing, bouncer, or car seat. These are wonderfully comforting places for a child to nap, but when they become necessary for sleep, then it's likely to cause a problem for the parent who must provide naptime services. These associations are usually so necessary to your child's sleep that they override every other reason or solution. Because these are complicated issues, each of these associations has its own chapter of solutions in other parts of this book. (Check the index for your topic.)

Problem: Health Problem

If any health issue is bothering your child, it can definitely affect his sleep. Allergies and asthma are two of the most common issues. Both of these conditions cause excess mucus secretion and swelling of nasal tissues, so they can make it difficult for your child to breathe comfortably when lying down. Colic, reflux, ear infections, and difficult bouts of teething are other conditions that can prevent a child from napping well.

Solutions

If your child suffers from any medical issues, then good naps are especially important for his health. If this is the case with your child, try to be flexible about using any solution that helps him sleep. Put aside any notion that your child must sleep in a certain way, and open yourself to the concept that any nap is better than no nap at all.

Children with upper respiratory issues often find relief napping in a more upright position, such as in a swing, hammock, sling, or bouncer seat. They are often soothed by motion and loud white noise. Experiment with various napping conditions to find the right answer for your child.

If your child takes regular medication, talk with your pharmacist about possible side effects of the medication. Sometimes these can cause wakefulness or sleep disruption, so you might change the dosage schedule to occur after naptime.

Problem: Overtired Due to Poor Night Sleep

There is a definite correlation between nighttime sleep and the length and the quality of daytime naps. Ironically, many children who don't nap well don't sleep well at night either. So if you can improve your child's nighttime sleep, he may take better daily naps.

Solutions

Solving night sleep problems is as complex as solving nap problems, but it is worth investing your time and energy, as your child will reap wonderful benefits from improved night sleep. I've written two entire No-Cry Sleep books about nighttime sleep, but here are a few highlights to get you on the right path. There are, of course, exceptions to every rule, but these main ideas can help most children sleep better at night:

- **Maintain a consistent bedtime and awaking time.** When you implement a set time for bedtime and wake-up time, you "set" your child's clock so that it functions automatically.
- **Aim for an early bedtime.** Babies and young children respond best with a bedtime between 6:00 and 7:30 P.M. Most children will sleep *better* and *longer* when they go to bed early.
- **Use light and darkness to set your child's biological clock.** Darkness pushes the biological "sleep" button, so dim the lights the hour before bedtime. Bright lights are alerting, so keep the room bright first thing in the morning and after your child wakes up from each daily nap.
- **Develop a consistent bedtime routine.** A consistent, peaceful bedtime routine allows your child to transition from the motion of the day to the tranquil state of sleep. A pleasant routine also acts as a cue to sleep and helps prevent bedtime battles.
- **Create a cozy sleep environment.** Where your child sleeps can be a key to quality sleep. Make certain the mattress is comfortable, the blankets are warm, the temperature is right, pajamas are comfy, and the bedroom is welcoming.
- **Help your child to be healthy and fit.** Too much TV watching, hours spent in a baby seat or swing, and a lack of activity prevent good sleep, both at naptime and bedtime. Children who get ample daily exercise fall asleep more quickly, sleep better, stay asleep longer, and wake up feeling refreshed. (Avoid activity in the hour before sleep, though, so your child isn't too revved up to sleep.)
- **Teach your child how to relax.** Follow a soothing prebedtime routine that creates sleepiness. Massage, yoga, stretching, reading, cuddling, or taking a warm bath are all good ways to help a child relax. Don't rush your presleep routine. Allow your child the time to get drowsy and relaxed.

Work with these ideas and you'll see improvements in your child's night sleep and in his naptime sleep, too.

Problem: Nap Routine Is Inappropriate, Inconsistent, or Nonexistent

Many times, the steps in the prenap routine are misaligned, so they don't aid in helping a child sleep. For example, if you get a child cozy in bed and then get back up to use the potty and wash hands, then your child may lose whatever relaxing state he acquired during your wind-down routine. Or, perhaps there is no prenap routine at all—a child engaged in play is suddenly whisked off to bed and expected to fall asleep. Without a good routine, it's natural for your child to resist a nap.

Solutions

A calming prenap routine sets the stage for sleep. A nap routine doesn't have to be long or complicated to be effective. What's important is that the routine is consistent from day to day and that it helps a child prepare for rest. Often a mini-version of the bedtime routine is best, since a child is already familiar and comfortable with the nighttime routine. So, as an example, if you read for twenty minutes before bed at night, you might read for ten minutes before a nap. If singing a lullaby occurs before bedtime, you might incorporate the same song or a similar one into your prenap routine.

If your child is old enough to understand it, you can create a naptime poster and hang it on the wall. It can have simple pictures (or photos of your child) that show the steps to naptime. That way, he can be involved in orchestrating the steps and be more accepting of the process. An older child can often be motivated with a nap calendar on which he can put a sticker each day after he wakes up from his nap.

Problem: Too Busy

Children have an incredible amount of energy. While most adults would love to have someone tell them to take a nap, most children resist even the idea of slowing down. Children may be afraid that if they take a nap they will miss out on "something."

Solutions

In order to help your child welcome his nap or rest time, avoid letting him get involved in a fun activity right before naptime. If your child is beginning to build a wonderful castle of blocks or has just opened a new tub of clay, she'll be reluctant to leave her

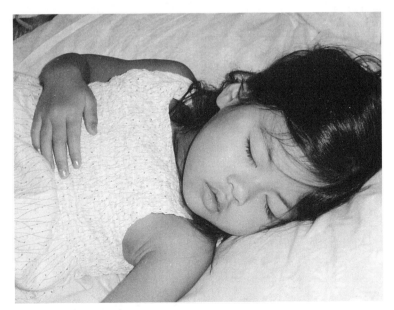

Adriane, three years old

project to take a nap. End any exciting activity a half hour or so before naptime. Help your child switch gears to something mellow. That way, when you move toward naptime, he won't fight you to continue playtime.

As you set your child up for a nap or quiet time, let him know what he can look forward to when he gets up. Tell him that by resting he'll have more energy to enjoy the afternoon plans. Explain what you'll be doing as he sleeps, and make it sound boring, such as "I'll be doing paperwork while you sleep." Saying this lets your child know he won't be missing anything exciting and that the fun stuff will happen when he wakes up.

Parents often pull a child away from a fun activity and take him to a boring crib or bed for naptime. You can make an easier transition by allowing him to nap in a more interesting place: create a fort out of a bedsheet and table with a pillow and blanket inside, put a sleeping bag on the floor in your office, or take a rest with your child. Few children will resist napping with mommy or daddy! (And the nap is good for you, too.)

Problem: Sneaky Micro-Naps

The very first stage of sleep can last as little as five minutes and can reduce the feelings of sleepiness brought on by homeostatic sleep pressure—it lifts the lid and lets the steam out just enough. If your child hits a tired zone and is lying on the sofa or going for a ride in the car, he may nod off for five or ten minutes. This micro-nap doesn't give your child the full benefit of a real nap but can be just enough to rejuvenate him and prevent him from being able to sleep when you put him in bed later for a nap.

Solutions

Avoid putting your child in a nap-inducing environment, like a ride in the car, at a time when he's likely to need a nap, unless you can leave him for a full nap. Schedule your days, when possible, so that you are home at naptime. Take advantage of carpools, baby-sitters, or schedule flexibility.

If it's impossible to avoid driving during your child's tired spell, then plan for a car nap. Turn on soft music or a white noise CD; keep a book, knitting, your computer, or paperwork in the car; and park to allow your child to take a real nap in his car seat. To make this safe, tilt your child's seat back (if it has this feature) or let your child rest with a child-sized neck pillow to prevent him from slumping over in his seat.

Keep aware of your own needs for sleep. If the car is set up to be a relaxing environment and you are sleep-deprived, then you may find that this isn't a good idea, as you don't want to be driving while drowsy. Stay safe and stay home, nap along with your child, or revamp your own sleep routines so that you aren't feeling so sleep-deprived.

Problem: Separation Anxiety

Separation anxiety can pop up at any age and become an obstacle to napping. Babies can suddenly have doubts when a parent leaves the room—*Where did mommy go? Is she gone forever?* This can prevent a baby from relaxing enough to fall asleep.

Separation anxiety is very common all the way up through the preschool years. It's a sensible fear: children who feel safe and secure when their caregivers are close by may feel unsettled when they must separate from them to lie alone in a dark room.

Solutions

Maintaining a consistent prenap routine is an important component to overcoming separation anxiety. It may help to use soft music during the nap as a transition from being with you to being alone. You might also encourage your child's attachment to a stuffed animal or special blanket; these are called "security objects" or "loveys," and they can give your child something to keep him company when you aren't there. Living company can be helpful too: a goldfish, turtle, or guinea pig as a bedside pet can provide some comfort to a child who doesn't want to be alone.

Reassure your child when she goes down for her nap that you are just down the hall and you'll see her as soon as she wakes up. Keep the door open or turn on a baby monitor and go to your child the minute you hear that she is awake. Sometimes a prenap discussion about where you will be while she is sleeping and then chatting about what is planned for when she wakes up can help encourage a peaceful sleep.

There is another way to solve naptime separation anxiety, if you wish. Set up a sleeping place close to wherever you will be spending the time. If you have a baby, use a cradle or stroller and park your baby next to you. An older child can be set up on the sofa or in a sleeping bag on the floor. Let him know that he can stay there as long as he keeps his eyes closed and rests, but if he gets up, he'll need to move to his bedroom.

One more way to solve naptime separation anxiety is to rest with your child. Play soft music, white noise, or an audiobook. Once your child is sleeping soundly, you can get up. That is, if you're not sleeping, too! If you *do* fall asleep, it's because your body needs that sleep. Research tells us that a short siesta midday is extremely beneficial for adults, so you'll be improving your own health and wellness with this daily rest.

Problem: *Thinks* He Has Outgrown Naps

Typically, children are ready to give up daily naps sometime between the ages of three and five *if* they get an adequate amount of nighttime sleep. However, a good percentage of children continue to need a daily nap; 65 percent of three-year-olds, 25 percent of four-year-olds, and 15 percent of five-year-olds still take naps,

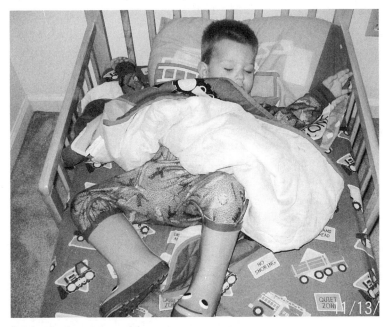

Benjamin, two years old

and it's very likely an additional percentage should be napping even though they aren't. Plenty of children believe that they are too old for naps; since many of their peers have stopped napping they think they should, too.

Solutions

Possibly the best way to contend with a child who thinks he has outgrown naps is to eliminate the word *nap* from your vocabulary. Instead of making the dreaded naptime announcement, offer your child a series of choices that lead her in your intended direction: "What books do you want to read today?" "Do you want to listen to music or birdsong?" "Which stuffed animal do you want to cuddle?" Older toddlers and preschoolers love having choices, and they are more likely to cooperate if they are making the decisions themselves.

You may want to implement the Hush Hour, described starting on page 120. Your child may be open to a rest time versus a sleep time. Teach him that it's important to have a daily break in order to enjoy the day and have more fun. Help him understand his own sleepy signs. "When you start to get grumpy that means your body is saying it needs you to take a break. You'll feel much happier when you get up."

You may want to invite your child to create a solution. Many parents suffer through the nap/no-nap war yet never think to include their child in coming up with the right solution. Preschoolers can often contribute valuable ideas, and if they are involved with creating solutions, they may be more likely to cooperate with the plan.

Problem: Has Truly Outgrown Naps

Sometime between the ages of three and five, most children are able to give up their daily naps without devastating effects. However, the journey between needing a nap every day and not needing naps at all is not a straight line. Most children spend months or even a year in an in-between place where they sometimes need a long nap, sometimes need a short nap, and sometimes just need a quiet rest break.

Solutions

Stick with a napping schedule for as long as you can. If you suspect your child may be outgrowing naps, then it's a good time to read the chapter "Shifting Schedules: Time to Give Up Naps?" Even after your child gives up naps for good, though, he can still benefit from a daily quiet time to recharge his energy. The ideas for creating this rest break, called a Hush Hour, are also described in that chapter.

Shifting Schedules
Changing from Two Naps to One Nap

....

See also: Catnaps: Making Short Naps Longer; The Nap Resister: When Your Child Needs a Nap but Won't Take One; Shifting Schedules: Time to Give Up Naps?

My seventeen-month-old son still takes two naps a day, but he's starting to fight me about naptime. Is he old enough to drop one of his naps? How do I know which one to drop?

Typically, between the ages of twelve and twenty-four months, toddlers switch from two daily naps to one. However, a year of difference between turning one and turning two is a very long span of time, and, developmentally, toddlers can be very different from one another. Half of all children change from two naps to one between twelve and eighteen months of age, but that means half of all children continue to have two naps a day at that age! This tells us that age alone is not the only factor to consider when changing your child from two daily naps to one.

Some toddlers can make you think it's time to make a change when it really isn't. They go on napping strikes for various reasons that are temporary and don't warrant a permanent schedule change.

The question of two naps versus one isn't about what your child thinks he wants. It's about the biological need for two naps versus one. Naps at different times of the day serve different purposes in brain development at different ages. Morning naps have more dreaming, or REM sleep, which is what makes them so important for infants and young babies, who require more REM sleep than older babies and toddlers because of the type of brain development that occurs in the early months. Since morning naps are the ones that usually disappear first, you don't want to rush the process if your child is still benefiting from this important sleep time. Your baby's moods and health can also be affected by dropping a nap too soon.

There is another consideration when deciding if your child is ready to make a nap schedule change. If you'll remember back to Part 1, we discussed the Volcano Effect (page 14), that is, the effect that the length of time that your child is awake from one sleep period to the next has on his mood and behavior. The older your child is, the longer he can go between sleep breaks without getting cranky. That's the reason that younger babies need to divide their day up with two naps but older babies can handle a full day with only one nap. Since there is a wide range of what's normal, it's important to study each child's behavior to see when he is ready to transition to one nap a day—and when he is able to handle the much longer awake periods from waking in the morning until naptime and from after nap until bedtime.

Napping Strikes

There are times when your baby resists napping for a while even though he still needs two good naps a day. Nap strikes can last a few days or a few weeks, and then your little one will suddenly start napping again. If you identify the reason for the strike and work around it, your child will revert back to his good napping schedule much sooner. Nearly any topic covered in this book can be the cause of a nap strike, so wander around the index and see if anything sounds like it fits your baby's pattern. A few of the common causes for these strikes and some quick solutions follow.

The Cause: *Learning to crawl, pull to a stand, or walk.* The eagerness to master new skills overtakes the tiredness factor, and your little one resists stopping this new activity long enough to relax and fall asleep.

The Solution: Give your child ample time to practice his new skills until about thirty minutes before naptime. At that time, amend activities to those that are less physical and less novel.

The Cause: *Illness.* If your baby has a cold, an ear infection, a difficult bout with teething, or other illness, it may make it difficult for him to fall asleep. He may be tired, but since he's unable to relax, he'll resist being put down for a nap. Another aspect of this is that when a child is sick, we often bend all the rules (as we should!) but then it's hard to get back on track.

The Solution: Identify the cause of your baby's discomfort and take measures to lessen the effects, such as raising the head of the bed, putting a humidifier in the room, using saline nose drops, or providing doctor-approved medication. Be flexible during illness, but get back to your usual schedule as soon as possible.

The Cause: *Sudden fears.* Perhaps something frightened your child one day at naptime, and it's sticking in his memory. Maybe the monitor battery died and your child cried for a long time before you knew he was awake, or your child fell out of bed during a nap. Your child may have a memory of the event the minute he sees his bed and be frightened about returning there to nap.

The Solution: It might help to change the routine or the furniture arrangement just a little bit. Stay calm and pleasant during the nap routine. It can be comforting if you introduce a new stuffed animal as a sleeping buddy. Have a brief, pleasant prenap routine.

The Cause: *Temporary interruption to routine.* An unusually busy week, having visitors, a later-than-normal bedtime, taking a vacation—these types of temporary interruptions to your child's usual routine can disrupt his body clock and cause him to be off-kilter for a few days.

The Solution: Jot down the best times for the day's touch points—wake-up, meals, naps, and bedtime—and stay within a half hour of your scheduled times. If you can do this for a week, you should be back on track.

The Cause: *Developmental change.* As children grow, their needs change in regard to eating and sleeping, and if we don't respond with a new schedule when needed, they will resist naptime.

The Solution: Watch your child for signs of hunger and tiredness in between usual meal and sleep times. See if he's hungry earlier than mealtime or not eating much when offered but is hungry later, and take note if he seems wide awake at naptime but dragging an hour later. Modify the schedule a bit and see if you can find a new eating and napping schedule that works better for your child.

Mother-Speak

"Recently we had relatives over for a weeklong visit. Their daughter takes one nap a day, so my son began to sleep when she did. After they left, I noticed that he was getting frustrated more often and fussing more than usual. Having only one nap a day was fine when we were busy with our visitors, but it caught up with him. He's now back to two naps a day and much happier. He definitely needs two naps to function properly."

—**Miranda, mother of
sixteen-month-old Joseph**

The Danger of Dropping a Nap Too Soon

The reputation that toddlers have that is known as the "terrible twos" is very likely caused by inappropriate napping schedules. There are a great number of toddlers who switch from two naps a day to one, or—heaven forbid!—drop naps altogether, many months before they are biologically ready. This can result in a devastating effect on their mood and behavior: the dreaded and horrible "terrible twos." For those parents whose children suffer the "trying threes" or the "fearsome fours," it's likely your child is misbehaving for the same reason: an inappropriate nap and sleep schedule. The good news is that a modification of the napping and night sleep schedule can make a wonderful and dramatic difference.

Making the Right Decision for Your Child

Children develop sleep maturity at different rates that can't be easily identified or measured, but you can take a good guess as to when it's time to switch from two naps to one nap and again when it is time to drop naps completely.

There are a number of issues to watch that can give you signs as to whether your child needs to hold on to that second nap. Some of the issues are purely a factor of age, and others are based on the individual needs of each child.

Watching Age and Hours

Let's start by revisiting the sleep chart that appears on page 8. It's always smart to take a look at your child's entire twenty-four-hour sleep pattern in order to have a clear picture of what is going on. It's also important to keep an eye on the typical awake-time span between sleep periods so that your child doesn't build too much homeostatic pressure and release his inner "volcano." It's also important to identify how much sleep your child gets on a typical night, because a shortage of night hours can be made up during naptime.

Signs That Your Child Needs Two Naps Daily

Just as children have different daytime personalities, they have different sleep personalities, too. But it's also important to consider all the typical signs that point to keeping a two-nap-a-day schedule. Review this list of signs that your child may be resisting the twice-a-day naps that he truly needs:

- Your child is under twelve months old or under twelve months adjusted age for babies who were premature at birth. (A small percentage of younger babies are ready to drop to one nap, but if any other signs point to keeping two naps, then try to maintain a two-nap schedule.)
- When you put your child down for a nap, he talks, plays, resists, or fusses for a while but always ends up falling asleep and sleeping for an hour or more.
- When you take your child for car rides during the day, he almost always falls asleep in the car.
- If your child misses a nap, he is cranky and fussy or acts tired until the next nap or bedtime.
- About three or four hours after waking from a nap, your child starts to get whiny, fussy, or easily frustrated or has tantrums.
- Your child is suffering from an ear infection, a cold, or painful teething or is undergoing a change in his life (such as a new sibling or starting day care) that seems to be disrupting his nap sleep.
- Your child often misses naps because you're on the go and not at home for naptime, but when you are at home all day, he takes two good naps.

Amelia, four years old

Signs That Your Child Is Ready to Change to One Nap Daily

If your child is physically ready to switch to one nap a day and you're continuing to try to enforce two naps, it is likely that it's creating tremendous stress for both of you. It's hard for anyone to fall asleep when they are wide awake, so your child won't be happy about being put to bed. And, of course, when he's unhappy, he cries, fusses, and complains—making each try-to-nap episode an unpleasant one for you, too. So, review this list to determine if it really is time to switch to one nap:

- When you put your child down for a nap, he plays or fusses for thirty minutes or more before falling asleep and then takes only a short nap or never falls asleep at all.

- Your child can go for car rides early in the day and not fall asleep in the car.
- When your child misses a nap, he is cheerful and energetic until the next nap or bedtime.
- Your child naps well for one of his naps but totally resists the other nap.

How to Make the Transition When Signs Point to Change

Instead of thinking in terms of *dropping a nap*, it's better to think in terms of a *schedule change*, as, in most cases, the new singular nap is really a melding of the two naps into one nap in the middle of the two previous times. Often this one nap is longer than either of the two previous naps but not quite as long as the two together.

The change from two naps to one nap is rarely a one-day occurrence. Most often there will be a transition period of several months when your child clearly needs two naps on some days but one nap on others, and on some days you'll have absolutely no idea if it's a one-nap day or a two-nap day! You have a number of options during this sometimes complicated transition time.

- Go with the flow, watch for your child's sleepy signs, and put your child down for a nap when those indications first appear. (Don't launch into a long prenap routine, as your child might pass though the sleepiness and get a second wind.)
- Keep two naps but don't require that your child *sleep* at both times; allow quiet resting instead (see "The Hush Hour," on page 120). This often works best as one longer late-morning sleeping nap and a shorter afternoon quiet-time rest period. If occasionally your child falls asleep during the second naptime, you can either let him sleep as long as he does—then be prepared to move bed-

time later—or gently wake him after an hour's sleep to preserve his usual bedtime.

- Choose a single naptime that is later than the usual morning nap but not as late as the afternoon nap. Keep your child active (and outside when possible) until about thirty minutes before the time you have chosen. At that time, give your child a healthy snack and begin a wind-down period and prenap routine. It may help to break lunch up into two parts, serving half of her lunch before her nap and half when she wakes up. For a few weeks she may be fussy or whiny that last hour or so. It's not her fault, so be patient as she adjusts to the new schedule.

- On days when a nap ends up being early in the day, move bedtime earlier by thirty minutes to an hour to minimize the length of time between nap and bedtime. Make sure your child's bedroom windows are covered so that early light doesn't wake him up too soon the next morning. Once your child is up for the day, keep the morning bright and busy until your child's usual midday naptime.

Sample Schedules

Every child is different, and every family functions in a unique way. Yet you may be wondering what your schedule should look like, so here are a few actual samples for you. I am not suggesting that you adopt any of these (unless they work for you and your child), but I have learned from experience that my readers like to have samples to help them figure out how their own child's day might look. Keep in mind that every day is different, so there is some flexibility in setting a schedule: watch the clock *and* your child.

Here are a few routines of children who take one daily nap and get an adequate amount of the important components of naptime, meals, snacks, and nighttime sleep. In between these cornerstone events, but not shown here, are hours of playtime and usual daily activities:

Samples of Toddlers' Daily Schedules*

	Ryan 16 months	Daisy 19 months	Siobhan 22 months	Preston 23 months	Charlene** 25 months
Awake	7:30	7:00	6:45	8:00	9:30
Breakfast	7:45	7:30	7:30	8:15	10:00
Snack	10:15	10:00	9:45	10:30	None
Lunch	11:30	12:00	11:00	12:30	1:30
Nap	12:15 2¾ hours	1:00 2½ hours	12:45 2 hours	1:30 1½ hours	2:30 2½ hours
Awake	3:00	3:30	2:45	3:00	5:00
Snack	3:30	Dinner 5:00	3:30	3:15	5:15
Dinner	5:50	Snack 6:30	5:30	5:30	Dinner 7:30 Snack 8:30
Prebed-time routine	7:15	7:30	6:15	6:45	9:00
Asleep***	7:45 11¾ hours	8:00 11 hours	7:30 11¼ hours	7:45 12¼ hours	9:30 12 hours
Total sleep hours (nap plus night)	14½ hours	13½ hours	13¼ hours	13¾ hours ·	14½ hours

*All times are rounded. (Life with children is not as exact as this chart appears!)

**Charlene has a later bedtime than is best for most children at this age, but she is able to sleep in late in the morning. This works with her family's schedule. She gets ample nap and night sleep and is a happy, healthy child, so it is perfectly acceptable.

***The number of night sleep hours shown does not necessarily mean unbroken sleep, since brief awaking between sleep cycles is normal, and because 47 percent of toddlers and 36 percent of preschoolers wake up *at least* once per night and need an adult's help to return to sleep. But *that* is another book . . .

Shifting Schedules
Time to Give Up Naps?

....

See also: Catnaps: Making Short Naps Longer;
Shifting Schedules: Changing from Two Naps
to One Nap; The Nap Resister: When Your
Child Needs a Nap but Won't Take One

> **My three-year-old never wants to take her
> nap. It takes me more than a half an hour
> to settle her down before she finally falls
> asleep. Is it time for her to give up napping?**

Children approach life with boundless energy and enthusiasm. They don't understand the biological benefits of sleep, so they see naps as an interruption to life—they don't feel naps are necessary. If it were up to them, they'd never sleep—day or night—until they simply keeled over. Leaving the decision to nap up to your child, then, is like allowing her to choose between vegetables or ice cream for dinner—just as ice cream would win hands down, your little one is unlikely to choose *sleep* over *awake*. Which leaves the decision entirely up to the grown-ups in the house.

There is a difference between a child who *needs* a nap and a child who would benefit from a nap. If your child falls in the "need" category, then I recommend you do everything you can to preserve that daily sleep. (For more tips read the chapter "The Nap Resister: When Your Child Needs a Nap but Won't Take One.")

If a nap is no longer a necessity for your child, then you might consider switching to a daily quiet time or Hush Hour (see page

112

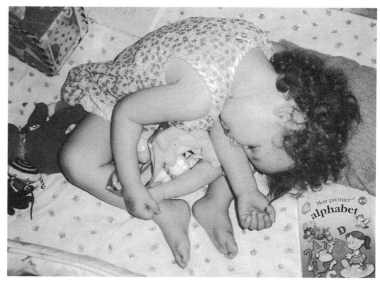

Nadine, two years old

Key Point

Approximately 85 percent of two-year-olds, 65 percent of three-year-olds, 25 percent of four-year-olds, and 15 percent of five-year-olds take a nap every day or almost every day. Biologically speaking, children are ready to give up daily naps sometime between the ages of three and five if they get an adequate amount of nighttime sleep. Regardless of the statistics or the averages, if your child *needs* a nap, he falls into the 100 percent category: 100 percent of the children who *need* a nap should take a nap.

Even if your child does fine all day without a nap, new research points to the fact that naps continue to be beneficial for human beings throughout their entire lives. So when you wonder, "When should my child give up naps?" The best answer may be "Never."

120). This will set up a restful environment in which your child can sleep on those days when she needs it or simply rest and rejuvenate on days when sleep isn't required. A Hush Hour can set up a healthy ritual that may serve your child for life.

Professional-Speak

"My belief, which is based on many years' experience, is that the single most significant contributing factor to early childhood social/emotional/behavior/learning problems is sleep deprivation.

"On any given day, a hugely disproportionate percentage of the children in most classrooms appear visibly exhausted. An exhausted child has less tolerance for frustration, less impulse control, shorter attention spans, and depressed cognitive abilities. They do not learn as easily or as much as a well-rested child learns, nor do they retain what they have learned. And they are just plain grouchy and hard to live with.

"I believe that children would perform better academically and develop stronger social skills if they continued to have midday nap/rest times until they are seven or eight years old."

—Linda Crisalli, professional early childhood educator and contributor, Child Care Exchange

---

How to Tell If Your Child Needs a Nap

If you watch carefully and if you know what to look for, you will be able to tell if your child *needs* a nap. The three lists that follow will help you know what to watch for. The first helps you determine if your child does, indeed, need a daily nap. The second will tell you if your child is weaning from taking a nap every day but that on some days he still needs to sleep, and the third list tells you if your child is ready to give up daily naps but would still benefit from a daily rest or quiet time.

Signs that your child needs a daily nap
- Responds in a positive or neutral way to naptime and falls asleep easily
- Resists the idea of a nap but eventually falls asleep and sleeps an hour or longer
- Wakes up in the morning in a good mood but gets whiny and cranky as the day progresses
- Has more patience early in the day but is more easily aggravated later on
- Cries more often or more easily in the evening than she does early in the day
- Demonstrates a deterioration in his coordination over the course of the day—begins falling down more, can't manage a puzzle as well, has trouble pulling up his pants
- Shows tired signs in the afternoon or early evening such as yawning, rubbing eyes, a slump in energy, or looking slightly glazed
- Late in the day, becomes wired up or hyperactive and won't settle down easily
- Often falls asleep in the car or when watching a movie
- When he misses his nap, the night's sleep that follows is disrupted
- Has a difficult time waking up in the morning or wakes up grumpy and stays that way for a while

Signs that your child is weaning from daily naps (he needs a nap on some days but just a rest period on other days)
- Usually has a consistent personality from morning until bedtime but on active days tends to become fussy in the evening

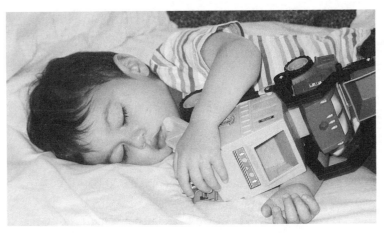

Austin, two years old

- Is generally in good spirits but can be overly grumpy or whiny on busy days or when his daily schedule is upset by visitors, playdates, or errands
- When she is put in a dark, quiet room for a nap, she often lies in bed a long time before falling asleep
- Seems to do alright missing one day's nap but after a few days of missing naps, starts to become more whiny or cranky
- Usually goes to bed at a reasonable time and sleeps well all night long

Signs that your child no longer needs a daily nap but still might benefit from a daily rest break or Hush Hour (described starting on page 120)
- Has a consistent personality from morning until bedtime, even on busy days
- Is generally in good spirits, with normal ups and downs throughout the day
- Learns new things easily and has an appropriate attention span for his age

- Goes to bed at a reasonable time and sleeps well all night long
- When put in bed for a nap, rarely falls asleep
- On the days when he naps, takes a long time to fall asleep that night, goes to bed much later than usual, or wakes up earlier in the morning
- Is typically healthy and doesn't suffer from many colds or other ailments
- Generally wakes up on her own and in a pleasant mood
- Sleeps the number of total sleep hours shown on the sleep chart on page 8 almost every night

Handling the Transition from One Nap to No Nap

Children aren't good nappers one day and nonnappers the next. There will likely be a transition period of several months (even as long as half a year) when your child clearly needs a nap some days but is fine without one on others. You have a number of options during this transition time:

- Schedule naptime on busy, active days. This can be a challenge because often the busier the day, the more a child needs a nap but the less likely there will be time for one! If you have an active day planned, try to work in a rest time at some point.
- If the timing works, set things up for a snooze in the car. Play soft music, your child's usual sleepy-time music, or white noise in the car. Provide a lovey, pacifier, or bottle if your child has one he usually sleeps with. If your child is a sound sleeper, you can transfer him to bed when you get home. If that would wake him, take advantage of the time by reading a book or resting in the car along with your child. (It's not safe to leave your child alone in the car.)

- Go with the flow from day to day, watch your child's sleepy signs, and arrange naps when needed. On days when it's not clear to you, set up a midday rest period and err on the side of relaxation just in case.

- Keep your child's regular naptime every day, but don't require that she *sleep*—allow quiet resting instead. For ideas on how to make this work, see "The Hush Hour" on page 120.

- On days when a nap is missed, move bedtime earlier by thirty minutes to an hour to get a longer night's sleep and to shorten the span from morning to bedtime. Make sure your child's room is dark so morning light doesn't wake him too early, and use white noise to mask any sounds that cause him to wake up before his usual waking time. The following day, keep the morning hours bright and busy to reset his body clock back to his usual schedule.

- On no-nap days when your child is fussy all day long and you find yourself getting short tempered, make a change to your usual meal schedule. Move dinner up by an hour or more and follow it with a very early bedtime—an hour or two early is acceptable once in a while when it's sorely needed by everyone. Don't narrate what you are doing—since your child can't tell time, he'll just

Mother-Speak

"I can't believe it! I actually did it—and it worked! The twins *both* missed their naps yesterday and were being absolute terrors. The crying, whining, and fighting were escalating. I was on the brink of losing it when I remembered your idea to move dinner earlier. So I threw together some macaroni and applesauce at 4:00 and sat them down to eat. Then we followed our regular after-dinner and before-bed routine. They were out cold by 6:30! I actually had a cup of hot cocoa and read a *grown-up book*. Ahhh."

—Tami, mother of three-year-old twins, Stephen and Stephanie

assume that it's dinner time and bedtime as usual. To prevent an early rising the next morning, make sure the windows are covered so the room remains dark when the sun comes up.

Are You Correctly Interpreting Signs of Tiredness?

If you try to put your child down for a nap *before* he is tired or when he is *overtired*, he won't be able to sleep. If you catch him tired, though, you'll have a good chance of having him fall asleep. Look over the signs of tiredness on page 88 and observe your child for these indicators or other unique signs.

Try to put your child down for a nap the moment you see any indication of fatigue to achieve the best nap. If you note the time that this occurs over a period of a week or so, you should see a pattern emerge. Once you can predict when tiredness will arrive, you can set up a daily nap schedule that suits your child's tired times perfectly.

In addition to signs of tiredness, also watch to see how long your little one has been awake. Remember that homeostatic sleep pressure builds and children can stay awake for only a certain period of time until they receive a biological pull toward a nap. Take a peek at the sleep chart on page 8 for sample awake-time spans between sleep periods to help guide your decision making.

Children grow and change, and their nap schedule should change with them. What's perfect today may be different from what is perfect next month or even on any given day—if it's particularly busy. Keep your eye on your child *and* on the clock.

Is Your Child Sneaking a Micro-Nap?

If you'll look back at the chart showing the many wonderful benefits, or "magic gifts," of sleep on page 12, you'll note that the very first stage of sleep can last as little as five minutes and can reduce feelings of sleepiness. If your child is lying on the sofa, perhaps watching television, or if he is sitting in the car, he may nod off for five or ten minutes. This micro-nap may be enough to rejuvenate him for the rest of the day.

The problem with these micro-naps is that they take the edge off just enough so that your child *cannot* fall asleep if you then put him to bed. But if your child actually needs more sleep than a few minutes, he won't receive the benefits that subsequent stages of sleep would bring him, such as an increase in alertness, improved motor skills, a boost to his immune system, regulation of his appetite, release of tension, restoration of energy, and a stabilizing effect on his behavior and mood.

To avoid having your child sneak in a micro-nap, keep an eye on him during the midafternoon for signs of fatigue. Avoid, if possible, car rides or TV time during his possible tired period. Either keep him active or set him up for a nap or Hush Hour.

Also, take a look at the sleep chart on page 8 and take note of the average awake time between sleep periods for your child's age group. For example, you'll see that a three-year-old typically can last six to eight hours before needing a break. That means if your three-year-old wakes up at 7:00 A.M., then between 1:00 and 3:00 would be a good time for rest. Keep your eye on your child *and* on the clock, and when the time is ripe, settle your child in bed for a nap or rest break.

 The Hush Hour

Every child can benefit from a daily nap, but sometimes there is nothing you can do to get your child to actually *sleep*. A dedicated nonnapper may convince you to stop any efforts for a rest break during the day. But day after day, week after week without a nap or rest break can result in a cumulative fatigue effect: a fussy, cranky child prone to temper tantrums, whining, and tears and the resulting spoiled afternoons for everyone.

Even when a child no longer sleeps, it's still a great idea to have a daily quiet-time break from noise and activity. I call this the *Hush Hour,* which is a nap substitute and good for:

- a child who is transitioning his schedule and moving toward giving up naps, therefore sometimes needs "half a nap"
- a child who is usually a good napper but on a given day is simply too wired, overtired, or involved to sleep
- a child who is ready to give up naps but would still benefit from a rest break in the middle of an active day
- a child who won't nap, can't nap, and refuses to nap but who lives with a parent who desperately needs that child to nap (to preserve said parent's patience, kindness, and dignity)

In any of these cases, a Hush Hour can provide a wonderful substitute for an actual nap. A child may eventually be past the need for a daily nap, but no child outgrows the benefits of a daily rest period. In addition, on that rare day when sleep is actually needed, a Hush Hour sets the stage for your child to fall asleep if she's tired.

The Hush Hour is magical in another respect. It can be a much-needed break for a parent or caregiver whose hours are filled with child-tending responsibilities. The Hush Hour allows you to leave your child in a safe, restful place so that you can do adult things or recharge your own battery. No parent should feel guilty or ashamed for wanting a brief break from constant child tending. No matter how much you love your child, no matter how much you enjoy his company, there is a grown-up person somewhere inside you that benefits from these brief breaks—times you can switch gears from Mommy or Daddy to

Continued

Man or Woman. The additional benefit of these breaks is that you can return to your child refreshed, or at least emotionally more relaxed, if you've used the time to catch up on necessary work or household tasks.

Mother-Speak

"I don't think the 'witching hour' ever really goes away. My two are in school full-time and have been without naps for two years, but they still have that time between 4:00 and 8:00 P.M. when it can be sheer craziness. Bouncing off the walls doesn't even grasp what it's like; ricocheting across the room racquetball-style might be a more accurate description. I hope it's not too late to initiate a Hush Hour, because I need it more than they do!"

**—Kathleen, mother of five-year-old David
and six-year-old Myles**

Why a Hush Hour

When naptime sleep is elusive, this is the time to institute the Hush Hour, a block of quiet time designed to refresh your child's mind and body. No matter the reason or the age, your child (and you) would definitely benefit from a daily respite from active play. The Hush Hour creates a calming break in the middle of the day that can act as a very effective buffer, providing enough emotional and physical refreshment for everyone to get through the rest of the day with a pleasant mood.

The Hush Hour becomes more effective when used on a regular basis and is most valuable when used at the same time every day. Try to create a daily ritual that includes a Hush Hour in the afternoon, perhaps after lunch, or when your child returns home from day care or school.

Components of the Hush Hour

The Hush Hour is a quiet, restful hour that takes place in a carefully constructed environment set up to encourage relaxation. Sleep is not required, but the setting often brings about a peaceful aftereffect, much as a nap would.

Setting

Choose a room that will host your child's Hush Hour. It might be your child's bedroom, your bedroom, or any other undisturbed room in the house. Choose a place that would work for a nap, just in case your child does fall asleep. If possible, remove toys and games from sight except for a few soft stuffed animals or your child's usual sleep-time lovey. (Toys will taunt and entice a child who is expected to be resting.)

If possible, regulate the temperature of the room so that it is neither too hot nor too cold. While individuals all have their own preferences, science tells us that the optimum temperature for most people is in the range of 60°F to 70°F (15.5°C to 21°C). If the temperature is too hot, a circulating fan can be helpful. In addition, the quality of the air can make a difference, too, particularly if a child has allergies, asthma, reflux, or the sniffles. Use a humidifier, dehumidifier, or air purifier if necessary.

Light

It's easier to feel relaxed in a dark room, since bright light is alerting to the human mind. Bright light signals playtime to a child. When it's time for a Hush Hour, it's helpful to use a darker room or draw the blinds.

There are some children who can sleep no matter how bright it is—they nod off even in the bright sunshine. However, light is the most powerful regulator of the human biological clock, so if your child is resisting a nap or a Hush Hour, you can aid the

Continued

transition to restfulness by closing the blinds and dimming the lights or turning them completely off.

Sound

An active mind is always looking for stimulation, so noisy distractions can prevent a child from resting. Conversely, a perfectly still and quiet room may create anxiety instead of restfulness. To combat both of these issues, fill the Hush Hour with gentle, relaxing music or white noise (a recording of rainfall, ocean waves, or static sound). This music or white noise can be comforting and also mask any noises that can distract your child, either sounds from within the house or those from outside.

As an alternative, you can have your child listen to an audiobook. Choose a pleasant story that isn't too exciting or frightening, nor one that your child finds boring. Your local library or bookstore carries many choices. Listening to a book is not only a wonderful way for a child to relax, but it can also create a valuable, enriching lifetime habit.

Surface

Even if your child can sleep *anywhere* when she's tired, it's best to create a cozy nest for Hush Hour since you'll be enticing a *nontired* child to rest, and a comfortable surface will help your cause. A bed is good, of course, but there is no scientific evidence to prove that a bed brings a better nap than any other comfortable surface. You want *your child* to be the one who finds his Hush Hour place cozy.

If your child find his bed too demanding of sleep and for this reason fights you about resting or if he relaxes more easily somewhere else, then choose the place that works best for him and you. A sofa is good. A sleeping bag on the floor can work, too. A cardboard box made into a Hush Hour nest or a cozy nook created behind the living room sofa are both good options. I work at home, and over the years all of my children have slept in my office, either on the sofa, in a stroller parked beside me, or in a sleeping bag on the floor near my desk. I discovered that they loved being near me and hearing the click-click of my computer keys. The comfort of having Mom so close by enabled them to get a nice, long rest (and allowed me a work session).

Smell

The aromas of lavender, chamomile, jasmine, sweet orange, and vanilla have long been used to entice relaxation. You can find scented pillows, stuffed animals, sprays, sachets, or potpourri. (Don't use candles in a room where a child will be left alone.) Scented oils can be used when washing bed linens. These pleasant, relaxing smells can enhance relaxation. They can also become a lovely cue for rest time for your child.

Food

The foods that your child eats prior to the Hush Hour can affect his ability to relax. Junk food, sugar, red meat, chocolate, citrus juice, simple carbohydrates (found in white bread and refined wheat products), fatty and greasy food, carbonated beverages, and caffeine can all prevent relaxation, so avoid these in the hour or two before Hush Hour.

There are foods that can induce a feeling of calm and even drowsiness, especially when eaten twenty to thirty minutes before rest time, so a well-planned lunch or snack can help your child relax. The best foods to aid rest are whole-grain carbohydrates, green leafy vegetables, cow's milk, soy milk, bananas, avocadoes, nuts, nut butters, seeds, and warm milk And, of course, the award-winning rest-inducing food: breast milk.

Continued

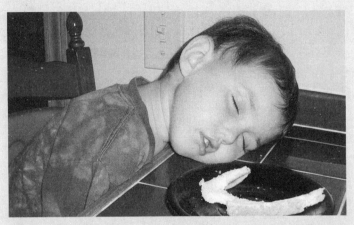

Zanon, four years old

Touch

Many children respond well to massage, back scratching, or gentle touch as a way to help them rest and relax. Massage is also proved to stimulate circulation, digestion, and neurological development. It can even boost the immune system. If your child suffers from any aches or pains, massage can bring relief. Massage can also increase bonding and connection between parent and child. If you can, build in a time for massage, back scratching, or cuddles as you set up your Hush Hour routine.

Ritual

The key to making Hush Hour work is to understand that it may not result in sleep but that an hour of peaceful rest can be wonderfully rejuvenating.

Decide on a time and place and create a simple daily routine leading up to Hush Hour, since a child will usually need to wind down a bit from playtime in order to relax. The pre-Hush Hour routine doesn't have to be complicated, but it should be consistent in its sequence of events and occur at roughly the same time every day. The routine might consist of having lunch, cleaning up, changing a diaper or visiting the potty, choosing a stuffed animal to rest with, picking out music to listen to, setting a timer, and settling into the Hush Hour nest.

One way to help your child relax is to assure him that the Hush Hour has a specific beginning *and* a certain end. You can do this by setting a white noise alarm, iPod, or clock radio to play for the entire one-hour period of time. Choose soft music or gentle sounds. Tell your child that he can get up when the music or sounds stop. This is a wonderful method because if your child actually does fall asleep, he will likely continue to sleep even after the sound stops.

Another Benefit of the Hush Hour

A hidden benefit of maintaining a regular Hush Hour routine is that it can help capture the reemerging nap. Many children stop napping for a while but then return to naps. This is sometimes a result of change in their daily schedule, bedtime, or awaking time. It may also occur in conjunction with a growth spurt or burst of physical development. No matter the cause, if your child doesn't take a break during the day, you'll never know if a nap lurks below the surface.

Mother-Speak

"Maddison is allergic to the word *nap*. I could be two counties away and mention the word, and she has a total meltdown! Tantrum, cries, stomps, you name it! I really love the Hush Hour idea and have started using it. Yesterday, I picked up Maddison after school, and she got in the car and asked, 'Mom, am I taking a Hush Hour?' She's accepted this in a way that she could never accept a nap. It's been a lifesaver for all of us."

—Patti, mother to Maddison, age four, and Mason, age two

Continued

The Hush Hour for a Baby

There are times when your baby should be napping but simply won't. If you put him in bed, he just plays or cries. If you take this as a cue to skip the nap, you not only get a fussy baby, you disturb the rest of the day's schedule or, worse, start a no-nap trend. A Hush Hour is important for maintaining a regular set pattern of play and rest.

The first step to a baby's Hush Hour is for you to create your own inner Hush. If you are tense, angry, or rushed, your baby will pick up on your emotions, and this will prevent him from relaxing. So, say to yourself, "This rest time is important for my baby. It will protect our schedule and make the rest of the day more peaceful. It will help him to fall asleep easier tonight at bedtime. I will relax and help my baby relax for this hour."

Set the stage for your baby's quiet time by going to the place where *you* feel most restful: your bedroom, your favorite rocking chair, a cozy sofa. Turn the lights down or off. Turn on some quiet, gentle music, white noise, or an audiobook (an adult book works wonders because of the comforting reader's voice and is a nice bonus for you). Then use whatever method relaxes your baby: his bouncer, swing, sling, or your arms. Maintain this mellow setting for about an hour. If your baby happens to fall asleep, try putting him in his bed (use the Pantley Dance, page 144), and he'll have his naptime. Even if he doesn't sleep, you will both feel more refreshed from this break.

The Hush Hour for a Toddler or Preschooler

Many active children come to dread the word *nap*. The moment you say it, they shift into high gear, as if by doing so they will push rest time away. They can become agitated in a way that prevents any hope of them falling asleep, even if they were extremely tired five minutes ago! The best solution is to ban the word from your own vocabulary and substitute it with "Hush Hour" or, more often, no title at all. Perhaps we should refer to it as *the hour that shall not be named*?

When you notice by the clock or by your child's behavior that rest time is needed, quietly go about setting one up. Typically, this occurs at the same time every day, often early afternoon, just after lunch, or when your child returns home from school.

Set up the Hush Hour room before you say a word to your child. For many children, this should be a place other than their bedroom, which is way too much like naptime. Create a cozy resting place with a blanket and pillow. Dim the lights or turn them off, and unplug any phones or devices that could disturb the peace. Turn on soft music or white noise. Sprinkle lavender scents and *then* bring your child to this restful room. Get your child settled and give him a massage or read a book, sing, or tell a story.

If you have a work space at home, you might try setting up a "nest" near your desk, as I did, and invite your child to lie near you. Many children love being close to mommy or daddy, and being invited to lie quietly for a bit in a special "nest" can become a pleasant ritual. Play soft music and concentrate on your work. If your child talks to you, don't engage conversation. A simple "Shhh, quiet now" might be all that's needed to help your child rest while preserving an extra hour of work time for you.

The Hush Hour for a Child

An older child might need more than music or white noise to encourage stillness during Hush Hour. You can either read a book to him (using a small book light or table lamp) or play an audiobook story. Listening to a story is much more restful than watching television, which requires eyes open and lights

Continued

on. An ongoing audio story can be a wonderful enticement for your child to look forward to Hush Hour every day.

If your child resists the idea of resting and isn't interested in story time, you can use a quiet playtime instead. Require your child to play quietly in his room or another contained space (one lacking active distractions) for an hour. Provide a special box of low-key activities to be used just for this hour, such as stuffed animals, books, puzzles, crayons, and paper. Put the box away at the end of each day's Hush Hour. Keeping the box unique to this time each day will keep it interesting.

When Your Child Won't Hush for Hush Hour

If at any time during the Hush Hour your child becomes anxious, upset, or too energetic to maintain the rest time, end your session. This is supposed to be restful, not painful! If possible, head outside for a walk, a bike ride, or a visit to the park. If you can't get outside, find an inside activity that requires some dancing, jumping, or climbing. A bit of physical activity followed by a glass of water and a healthy snack can get the blood pumping and push your child past that biological mid-day slump. This will boost your child's mood (and likely yours, too) for the rest of the day.

When to Discontinue the Hush Hour

Even if your child functions beautifully without a nap and you are comfortable with having him give up naps completely, there is no harm in continuing to keep a Hush Hour built into your child's daily schedule. Every human being benefits from a brief break in the middle of the day, so if you and your child enjoy the peace and tranquility of a Hush Hour, then, by all means, continue the practice for as long as it works for your family, even up through the school years.

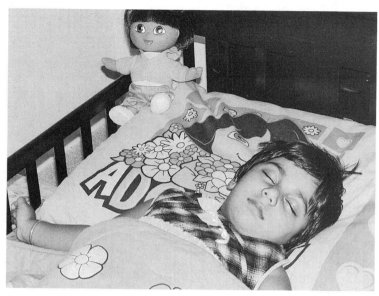

Isabella, two and a half years old

Sample Schedules

Every child is different, and every family functions in a unique way. Yet I know that many of you may be wondering what your new schedule should look like, so here are a few actual samples for you to review. I am not suggesting that you adopt any of these schedules (unless they work for you), but I have learned from experience that my readers like to have these samples, so I've included some here.

As you review these sample schedules, keep in mind that family life is fluid and every day is a little bit different, so there is flexibility in setting a schedule. It can help, though, to have a guideline for your child's daily routine. Here are a few sample schedules from children who take one daily nap or a Hush Hour and get an adequate amount of the important components of naptime, meals, snacks, and nighttime sleep. In between these cornerstone events (but not shown) are hours of playtime, of course!

Samples of Children's Daily Schedules*

	Alyssa age 2½	Ethan age 3	Sofia age 4 pre-school	Mya age 5 kinder-garten	Hector age 6 kinder-garten
Awake	7:00	8:30	7:30	6:15	7:30
Breakfast	8:00	9:15	7:45	6:30	7:45
Snack	10:00	11:00	9:45	9:00	10:00 (at school)
Lunch	12:00	1:30	1:00	11:30	11:45 (at school)
Nap or Hush Hour	1:00 (nap) 2 hours	3:00 (nap) 1½ hours	1:30 (Hush) 1 hour	12:30 (nap) 1¼ hours	3:00 (Hush) 1½ hours
Awake	3:00	4:30	2:30	1:45	4:30
Snack	4:00	Dinner 5:30	3:15	2:30	4:45
Dinner	5:30	Snack 7:00	5:00 Snack 6:45	6:00	6:00 Snack 7:00
Prebed-time routine	7:00	8:00	7:00	7:00	7:15
Asleep**	8:00 11 hours	9:00 11½ hours	8:00 11½ hours	7:30 10¾ hours	8:30 11 hours
Total sleep hours (nap plus night)	13 hours	13 hours	11½ hours + 1 Hush Hour	12 hours	11 hours + 1½ Hush Hours

*All times are rounded. (Life with children is not as exact as this chart appears!)
**The number of night sleep hours shown does not necessarily mean unbroken sleep, since brief awaking between sleep cycles is normal, and because 47 percent of toddlers and 36 percent of preschoolers wake up *at least* once per night and need an adult's help to return to sleep.

When Your Child Resists Both Naps *and* a Hush Hour

If naps are *impossible* and you can't even manage a Hush *minute* let alone an hour, your child may buzz through the day with high energy but run out of steam after dinner (when it's much too late for a nap). As a consequence, there will be more stubbornness, more tantrums, more crying and—ironically and amazingly—a battle against bedtime, since overtired children are too wired to sleep. Have heart. There are still things you can do to help your child get a midday break and take the edge off the fussiness.

If your child resists a midday rest, you can be very creative and trick him into being still for an hour. Here are a few ways to pull this off:

• Visit your local library once a week and fill a box with plenty of new books. (They are *free*, you know!) In the afternoon, when your child seems to be sagging a bit or getting fussy, take a stack of books to the sofa, give your child a sippy cup of milk, and read for a while. Not only does this keep your little one still and quiet, it's the best thing you can do for your child's future academic success.

• If the weather permits, take your child out for a stroller-walk. Jogging strollers are made for children up to five or six years old, so this idea can work for several years. Double strollers are great if you have a toddler and a baby. Most children love having a stroll, and the quiet rolling and sightseeing can be very relaxing. If you are a bicycler, invest in a bike trailer for your child. (Some convert from bike trailer to jogging stroller.) You may find that your child's afternoon fussy time turns into the highlight of your day!

• A wonderful way to handle your child's afternoon grumpy time is to turn it into an opportunity for love and bonding. Really! If you notice that your child is acting tired, whiny, and fussy, take twenty minutes or more and dedicate it to some one-on-one playtime with your child. Pull out the crayons and paper, plastic animals, or building blocks and give your child some personal attention. In most cases, this will magically wipe away any negative emotions and turn your child into her happy self again.

• As a parenting professional, I couldn't possibly in good conscience give you this next suggestion, but as a mother of four, I would be remiss if I didn't. So, I'll quote the brilliant Dr. Will Wilkoff, a pediatrician and author of *Is My Child Overtired?*, who will tell you what to do after lunch, when your child arrives home from day care or school, or at any point in the late afternoon when your patience cannot handle another whiny meltdown:

> Like many pediatricians, I feel that the television-viewing habits of our children are seriously interfering with their health. The physical inactivity associated with watching TV is already taking its toll on the fitness of both children and adults and is a major contributor to health problems such as obesity and diabetes. However, if your child is not buying the siesta concept despite your best efforts at creating a mellow and rest-inducing atmosphere, "the tube" may be the answer. As distasteful as it may be for me to suggest such a thing, you might try sitting your child down in front of a nonaction video for an hour or so. At least one study has demonstrated that television viewers burn only slightly more calories per hour than they do when they are sleeping. Although this may not be good news for those of you hoping to lose weight by watching television, it does demonstrate that "tubing out" is very similar to sleep and may provide your child with a chance to recharge her batteries.

• If your child won't slow down during the day, it may help to put him to bed at night earlier. Experiment with an early bedtime that gives him ample sleep without waking too early in the morning. To do this, make sure the bedroom is dark until an appropriate wake-up time. Watch for morning noises that rouse your child before he's ready to awaken. A white-noise machine or clock radio set to fill the room with soothing sounds or music about an hour before your child normally wakes up may charm him into sleeping a bit longer in the morning.

Nap or No Nap, Hush or No Hush, Remember These Important Ideas

Whether your child naps, takes a Hush Hour, or flies through the day without either of these, remember these key points to help your child be happy and healthy:

- Maintain a consistent bedtime every day.
- Make sure that your child has an adequate amount of night sleep.
- Provide your child with a daily diet of healthy foods.
- Encourage your child to be physically active every day.
- Take your child for regular health exams.

Changing from In-Arms Sleep to In-Bed Sleep

See also: Naptime Nursling: Falling Asleep Without the Breast, Bottle, or Pacifier; Swinging, Bouncing, Vibrating, or Gliding: Making the Transition from Motion Sleep to Stationary Sleep

I always rock my three-month-old daughter to sleep in my arms and then hold her while she naps. She's getting bigger and heavier, and it is very tiring and stressful for me. Plus, I would love to do some non-baby things while she sleeps! But if I try to put her down, she wakes up, so I either have to hold her for her entire nap or skip a nap completely. How can I move her from sleeping in my arms to sleeping in her crib?

Your daughter isn't the only baby who is cradled in a loving adult's arms as she sleeps—studies show that over 65 percent of infants fall asleep this way, so she's clearly in the majority. It's easy to see why: for a baby, being held by a parent or caregiver is the closest thing to the experience of being inside the womb—the cozy, secure place where your baby began life. In a perfect world, we'd carry all babies as often as they'd like and allow them to sleep in the comfort of our arms. But arms get tired, and there are many tasks that need to be done with two of them, such as cooking, working, tending to other children, exercising, showering, or clipping your toenails. In addition, since babies require 100 percent of our attention when they are awake, it can be tremendously challenging when they also require 100 percent of our attention when they are asleep. For most parents, helping a baby to take adequate daily naps in his own bed is an important and essential accomplishment.

Key Point
Important Notice for Those Who Hold Sleeping Babies

If you really love having your sleeping baby in your arms and your daily schedule allows this pleasure, then continue on as you are with my blessings. Don't change what works for you and your baby because someone else told you that you should. If your baby is having long, restful naps in your arms or sling and you are happy holding him, go ahead and enjoy this precious, fleeting time in your life and his.

Don't change what works today for some fear of future problems. It will likely be no harder or easier for your baby to make a change now or later, but it will be easier for *you* when you are truly ready and motivated to create change.

Babies are babies for a very short time—blink and they are off to college. So, if you are happy with today's in-arms nap routine, then *carry on*!

There will come a time when you feel ready to move your baby from your arms to his bed. It might be today, next month, or even next year. The right time is different for everyone, and *your right time* is when you should make that change—without guilt or anxiety. Read this chapter and apply these gentle no-cry sleep solutions when *you* are ready to make a change from in-arms naps to in-bed naps.

What Does Sleeping "Like a Baby" Mean?

Babies are not born with the ability to sleep like adults. Babies sleep like babies: they often require wooing to sleep, and then they wake frequently and nap erratically. According to sleep expert Dr. William Dement, who is considered to be the world's leading authority on sleep, it can take a long time for a baby's biological clock to mature. Dr. Dement says, "As the weeks go by, the baby starts sleeping longer and being awake longer. This is caused by the consolidation of sleep periods. Then, around *the fortieth week*, the baby has started waking and going to sleep about the same time each day. His biological clock becomes in tune with the twenty-four-hour day."

This means that it may take your baby nine or more months to transition from "newborn sleep" to "baby sleep." This is part of the reason why some professionals refer to the first nine months outside of the womb as the second half of gestation. During this transitional time, your baby will have short sleep cycles and may need your help to fall asleep and stay asleep. This delicate and irregular sleeping pattern is why so many parents resort to holding their sleeping babies to achieve their daily naps.

Babies who co-sleep at night often require in-arms naps during the day because they are unfamiliar with sleeping alone. These highly tactile sleepers need special conditions to help them sleep alone, either for night sleep or for naps.

Take heart! Babies do outgrow the need to be carried to sleep eventually. And even before that, we can do many things to move the process along. It is the womblike environment that helps babies to be calmer and sleep better. While in-arms naps are the ultimate womblike environment, there are many other ways to create a cozy sleep-inducing place for your baby and transition him from in-arms naps to in-bed naps.

This chapter will present a variety of ideas for you to review and choose from. Remember that there are no "must-dos" or even "should-dos"—every baby is unique, and every parent has distinctive needs and goals as well. I suggest that you read through all these ideas and those in the rest of this book, pick out the solutions that appeal to you, and create a written nap plan (see page 27). Follow through on your plan with purpose, dedication, and a super-colossal dose of love and patience.

Set the Scene for Naptime

When your baby sleeps in your arms, it's likely that there are no other conditions necessary for him to sleep. It won't matter what time it is, how dark it is, or if you are standing on a street corner in New York City. When you are ready to encourage your baby to sleep in a location other than your arms, you'll need to be aware of many other facets of napping that you've not had to consider before. No matter which solutions you choose, it can help to follow these tips, since your baby will welcome sleep easier if you set up the right conditions for a nap to happen.

- Plan and follow a nap schedule based on the information in the sleep chart on page 8.
- Learn to identify your baby's sleepy signals (pages 44 and 88) and put him down for a nap the minute you identify his signs of fatigue; don't let your baby get overtired.
- Watch the clock and your baby equally to determine the best nap times.
- After your baby wakes up, keep him active and exposed to bright light.
- Tone down the activity, lights, and noise about a half hour before naptime to help your baby wind down and prepare for sleep.
- Keep the napping area dimly lit and free from loud or jarring noises.
- Aid sleep with the consistent use of soft lullabies or white noise.
- Try swaddling for naps if your baby is a newborn.

- Make certain your child is sleeping safely.
- Choose the solutions that work best for you and your child.

Mother-Speak

"My doctor said that holding my newborn for naps makes her rely on me. This is the most ridiculous thing I've ever heard! Of *course* she relies on me—she's a four-week-old baby, for goodness sake!"

—Melissa, mother of four-week-old Hannah

Make the Crib Cozy and Comfortable

Before we talk about the ways to transition your baby from arms to bed, it can help to get the bed ready for your baby. First, consider how your baby is snuggled in your arms for sleep. His position, the tactile experience, the sounds, the smell, and the feel are all very different from the experience of lying alone on a big, flat crib mattress. In addition, when your baby is in your arms, you are as close as you can get to each other. Even if the crib or cradle is two inches from your chair (it might as well be half a block as far as your baby is concerned), he can hear you and sense you but not feel you, and this may prevent him from relaxing enough to sleep. If you can change the crib setting to duplicate some of the components of an in-arms nap, then you have a much better chance of having your baby accept this napping-place alternative.

Even if your baby willingly sleeps in the crib for nighttime sleep, you may have to consider modifications to make the crib more acceptable to your baby for daytime naps. There are a number of ways to modify the crib so that it is more inviting to your baby:

- Investigate the purchase of a baby hammock or swinging cradle, particularly if your baby is a newborn. Many are attached to a spring assembly that creates movement when your baby moves. These beds provide the soft, flexible surface that a crib lacks and are a natural for babies who love to sleep in arms.

Some of these beds are intended for infants, so older babies may quickly pass the weight limit. Others can accommodate a child up to about age two, and there are hammocks that are made for children up to about eighty pounds. The design should be age-appropriate and protect your little one from rolling over or falling out. Some have a built-in safety harness strap system similar to those in car seats, and some have side bolsters to secure newborns or tiny babies. Those for older children hang very low to the ground.

• Changing the angle of the mattress can be helpful, especially if your baby has colic, allergies, asthma, reflux, or recurring ear infections or is a fussy sleeper. A crib wedge lifts the head portion of the mattress, changing it from a flat surface to one with a slight upturned angle. A wedge that is positioned under the crib sheet lifts the head of the bed much like the angle of your arms. Some wedges contain a fastener to prevent your baby from sliding or rolling and provide additional tactile assurance.

• As an alternative, you can place a piece of wood under the *mattress* at the head of the bed, or two-inch furniture lifts under feet at the head of the crib. (No matter what method you choose, be sure the crib remains completely stable and that you don't alter the fit of the mattress within the crib at all.)

• Investigate the use of a crib positioner to keep your baby snugly hugged. These are two foam bolsters connected with a fabric valley and made specifically for keeping an infant in a back-sleeping position. While these have not yet been approved by safety organizations, they are very popular, so keep your eye out for new versions that earn the stamp of approval, or check with your health care provider for a recommendation.

• Experiment with the placement and positioning of your baby within the crib. Many babies prefer being wedged up into the upper corner of the crib so that they can feel something on the top and side of them, instead of free-floating somewhere in the middle. Other babies like to feel something near their feet, so placing your baby toward the very bottom of the crib is better.

• Once your baby is past the newborn stage, you can put a small, baby-safe stuffed animal in the crib. Often the best place for this toy is beside your baby's hips, legs, or feet, since many babies like to feel something beside them as they sleep. Another option is to roll a receiving blanket into a tight sausage shape and tape it securely. Place it next to your baby's legs or under your baby's knees to create a more natural sleeping position.

• If your baby seems lost in the big crib, place a small travel cradle, portable baby hammock, or Moses basket *inside the crib*. This smaller space is cozier than a big crib. (Make sure it is stable and won't tip. Use one designed with a box-type bottom, not legs.)

• An alternative is to use an infant bed nest (a U-shaped device designed to protect a baby who is co-sleeping with adults) or a crib spacer (used to divide a crib in two sections). Of course, you should always check the safety information on any baby product that you buy. The additional advantage to creating a smaller bed-within-the-bed is that once your baby is accustomed to the cradle or nest inside the crib, he will likely take to the crib itself once the cradle is removed.

• Invest in a quality crib mattress or padded crib mattress cover. Many of the standard mattresses that come with cribs are hard, stiff, and plastic-coated, making for an uncomfortable sleeping surface for any baby, let alone one who prefers the soft, yielding feel of being held while she sleeps. Shop around for a mattress that has a superior cushion, such as a foam core. You can also find padded or quilted crib mattress pads that are safe yet softer than the mattress alone would be. Some of these covers are short-pile, hypoallergenic lambswool or sheepskin, or flannel. Placed *under* a regular sheet, they can make the mattress much cozier. (Don't put a regular bed quilt in the crib as it is too bulky and can bunch up and create a breathing hazard. Purchase sheets, blankets, and covers intended for a baby crib and that fit securely around your mattress.)

• Use soft crib sheets, such as those made of fleece, flannel, terry cloth, jersey knit, or chenille. These fabrics are soft and warmer to the touch than traditional sheets and less jarring when you first lay your baby down. The soft fabric appeals to your baby's sense of touch and can help him relax in bed.

• To ease the transition from your cozy arms to the crib, warm the bed surface before naptime. There are a number of ways to do this. You can lay a warm towel (just out of the dryer) on the baby's spot while you get her ready for bed. You can use a heat pack, a hot water bottle, or a heating pad (set on the lowest setting) on the surface of the bed while you are preparing baby for a nap. Always remove the heat source and test the temperature of the surface before you lay your baby down.

A wonderful choice for a bed warmer is a microwavable aroma-therapy heat pack scented with lavender, vanilla, or chamomile. This can be particularly effective because it works with two of your baby's senses, and it creates a lovely cue for sleep. The first time you use this idea, test it out in your own bed to make certain it doesn't create too strong of an odor on the sheets. Keep in mind a baby's sense of smell is more pronounced than yours—it should leave just a faint, barely-there fragrance.

• Take advantage of a baby's desire for soothing sounds. Let your baby fall asleep and take his entire nap to gentle lullabies or white noise, such as recordings of ocean waves, rainfall, the hush of wind, or the sound of a heartbeat. A radio set to a low-key, talk-only station is also a wonderful "white noise" choice for a baby because of the soothing sound of human voices.

• Keep your baby's napping room dimly lit. Close the blinds and put night-lights out of your baby's direct line of vision. When a baby is a good sleeper or sleeps in your arms, he can probably nap anywhere, but in bed, he'll likely sleep better and longer in a darkened room.

• Let your baby have several quiet play sessions in his crib during waking hours. Stay with him and engage his interest. Point out the things he sees. Introduce new toys. Let him see you as a part of the crib experience so that he gets a happy feeling there and becomes familiar with the setting. This way, when he is put in his crib for naptime, it won't be a foreign place but one that carries memories of fun times with you, which can help him accept it as a place for naps.

• Dress your baby comfortably for sleep. If your baby is an infant, consider swaddling her for her nap, as a swaddled baby can often transfer from arms to bed easier than one in a loose blanket. If your baby doesn't like to be swaddled or is older, he could wear a blanket sleeper, an armless sleep sack-style sleeper, or comfortable, soft clothing.

• If the pajamas don't have foot covering, add socks, as bare feet touching the cooler air or mattress can cause your baby to wake up. (Take caution that your baby isn't overdressed and hot, as overheating can be dangerous.)

• Put your baby in a nighttime-quality diaper so that wetness doesn't shortchange his naptime.

The Pantley Dance

It's extremely common for a baby to fall asleep in someone's arms but then to wake up the moment she is put into the crib. The reason for this is that the conditions are drastically different between being cradled in warm, cuddling arms and lying on the flat, still surface of a bed. The difference is so dramatic that baby instantly wakes up and protests. So, instead of "putting down" your baby, try gently *gliding* your baby into bed using the Pantley Dance. This is not just a method of preventing the waking, but it can also help set up for other ideas to make crib sleeping easier to adapt to, since it allows your baby to settle to sleep, thus giving him practice and experience sleeping in his own bed.

Step One: Prepare your baby's bedroom and bed using ideas from the previous section, "Make the Crib Cozy and Comfortable." (For example: dress your baby for sleep, shut the blinds, turn on the white noise, set up the nest, and warm the sheets.)

Step Two: Hold your baby as usual and allow him to *become very sleepy* in your arms. Let him settle into the state where he is relaxed but not limp-limbed and asleep. This is when you'll begin the "dance" to glide your baby into bed. For the first few times, you might wait until your baby's eyes are closed and he is just drifting off to sleep. After a few days of practice, make the move sooner, and a few days later, sooner still.

Experiment with the position in which you hold your baby in your arms. If you now hold him upright or belly-to-belly with you and then you lay him flat on his back, the flip-over, radical change in position might contribute to his waking. Try holding him in a more reclined, upward-facing position, similar to how he'll be lying in the crib.

Step Three: Begin to softly sing, hum, make shush-shush sounds, or talk quietly, as you rock, bounce, pat, or jiggle your baby in your arms. Create a full sensory experience of movement and sound. Do this for a few minutes and then stop and remain perfectly still and quiet for a few minutes. Then resume movement. Continue to alternate movement and stillness with sound and quiet as you carry your baby to her bed. Alternate a few steps of movement, then stop and be still. Repeat.

Continued

Some babies do well if you alternate sound and quiet along with movement and stillness, but others will need for you to keep singing or humming consistently during both movement and stillness; the sound creates a common thread for both experiences. Experiment to find out the best combination of movement and sound for your baby.

If you use the same song, humming style, or monologue each time you put your baby down for a nap, this will become a key part of your routine and become a signal that it is time for sleep. (This method can also be used at bedtime.)

Step Four: Continue the Pantley Dance, alternating movement and sound with stillness and quiet (or stillness plus sound) as you lay your baby down. Place your baby in the crib so that only her feet touch the mattress, then pause. (You may need to keep humming at this juncture.) Then begin movement again and slowly ease her to the mattress, from bottom to top: feet, legs, bottom, back, and head.

Step Five: Gently touch your baby with your free hand. (You might try rubbing, patting, or simply putting pressure on his chest, belly, legs, or head.) Move the other hand out from under your baby. Continuing your song, do a round or two of alternating pat or rub, and then be still. Then remove your second hand.

With physical contact broken, continue your song but slowly reduce the volume. Prior to this you should have had your white noise or lullaby turned on, so it is now background noise.

If your baby wakes or fusses—either now or twenty minutes from now—put both hands on him and jiggle or pat while you continue the same song or humming as before to see if he will settle back to sleep.

Step Six: Set up a baby monitor or stay close to your sleeping baby; if he wakes up before a full naptime, you will use the same resettling technique to help him fall back to sleep and prolong the nap. The minute you hear your baby waking up, return quickly and resume the same patting and quiet humming or singing sounds. (Do take care that your baby isn't making noises in his sleep. If so, don't rush to his side. Wait and listen.) Note: If at any point your baby fully wakes and begins to cry, pick him up and start again at Step One. You want this process to develop into a soothing presleep routine and not a trigger to cry.

It will take persistence, but you can build this into a new bed-sleeping ritual. This gentle dance will teach your baby that the transition from arms to bed is a peaceful, pleasant experience and not one to be feared or resisted.

Mother-Speak

"My three-month-old, Sammy, would *never* let me put him down for a nap without immediately crying, so I held him for every nap. I used many of your crib set-up ideas and have been doing the Pantley Dance for about a week, and today was a milestone day! He took a two-hour nap in this crib! Two hours! Alone! I barely knew what to do with myself! Sorry for all the exclamation points, but it's a very big day around here!"

—Jenny, mother of three-month-old Samuel

If you wish, after a few weeks, the Pantley Dance can turn into your *prenap routine.* You can "dance" with your *awake* baby, and your little one can actually do all of his falling asleep in the crib.

However, *you do not have to make your baby fall asleep alone if you choose not to*. A large percentage of babies are parented to sleep for every nap and every nighttime sleep. According to a major survey done by the National Sleep Foundation, more than two-thirds (68 percent) of parents say they stay with their babies until they are asleep. All of these children learn how to fall asleep on their own—over time. There is no scientific evidence that a baby who puts himself to sleep will nap better or that he will be a better lifetime sleeper than one who requires a parent's assistance. The decision on this point is entirely up to you.

It might take a week or two of rehearsal to master the Pantley Dance, and it may take time for you to find the right combination of bed preparation, movement, and sound. It also may take time for your baby to adjust to the change in his current routine, since whatever you have been doing (even if it's holding, nursing, or rocking) has been your baby's "routine." Changing from in-arms

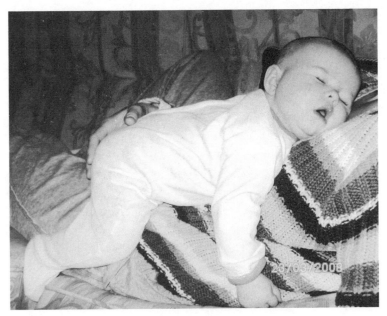

Leilah, four months old, on Mummy Rebecca

to in-bed naps is something that will require adjustment on his part.

If you have bedtime issues with your baby, the Pantley Dance can be a useful technique for bedtime, too. By using the same method for both, you may see quicker results since the routine will be consistent for all sleeping times. However, if your baby goes to sleep and sleeps all night just fine, then don't change a thing in that arena!

The ideas that follow can be used either in conjunction with the Pantley Dance or in combination with some of the bed-preparation ideas. In addition, any one idea can be used alone. So review the ideas to choose any you wish to try, and don't be afraid to add or change things if they don't seem to be working after a few weeks of consistent effort.

Invite a Sleepy-Time Buddy to Bed

When your baby leaves your arms for an empty bed, it can feel like something is missing, thus your baby might instantly wake up or startle awake soon after you put her down. It can help to have something comforting next to her when she leaves your arms.

If your baby is past the newborn stage, you can use a small lovey as a bedmate, such as a small stuffed animal or tiny baby blanket. It should have no potentially removable or loose pieces and should not be filled with beads that could escape a chewed seam. Many companies make loveys especially for infants, so they are free of buttons or fringe and are small enough for a baby to handle safely. Some even include a small white-noise or heartbeat mechanism built inside, such as a Prince Lionheart Slumber Bear. The Warm Buddy Company makes a plush bear that features a hidden compartment for a microwavable warming pad. Other products feature aromatherapy pillows filled with lavender. (Check the safety information on any of these products to make sure they are safe for your baby.)

Research shows that a baby can recognize her own parents by scent. You can soothe your baby's senses by leaving a bit of your warmth and scent with her in a lovey toy or baby blanket. Tuck this lovey or blankie into your shirt or cuddle it between you and your baby during the time you are preparing for nap, and then place it in the crib with her when you lay her down. It's best if you use this lovey only for sleep time so that it becomes one of your baby's sleep cues. If your baby drags around his blankie or carries his lovey all day, then it can be a comforting security object but may lose its power as a sleep aid.

Lest you worry, a lovey does *not* take your place, as if any toy could. This is a transitional object that comforts your baby in your absence and is common among happy, well-adjusted children. Some children never adopt a lovey but can be comforted by its presence during the switch from arms to crib sleep.

Create a Midway Step

If your baby totally resists your efforts to have him sleep in a crib, you can use a step-by-step process, changing to a temporary nap location now and then to the crib a few months from now when his sleep biology is more stabilized.

Many in-arm sleepers will adjust to having naps in a cradle-type swing or reclining stroller much easier than in a crib. You can use the Pantley Dance to transition your baby from your arms, exactly as previously described. Infants, in particular, will often accept this alternative to your arms because it provides many of the conditions that duplicate the womb: a soft, yielding surface, movement, and sound. Another advantage to using a swing or stroller is that you can keep your baby close to you during naptime. Many in-arms sleeping babies will snooze better if they can hear you nearby.

With either of these choices, you can help your baby take a nice, long nap even if he wakes up midway. If he starts to awaken before his nap is complete, just turn on the swing or roll or jiggle the stroller to coax your baby back to sleep to finish his nap.

When the time comes to transition your baby to a stationary bed, you can use the ideas in the chapter "Swinging, Bouncing, Vibrating, or Gliding: Making the Transition from Motion Sleep to Stationary Sleep." While you will have to face another nap transition from the swing or stroller to a crib, most parents find that it is a lifesaving middle step for a baby who needs to be held for every nap. This change can also help you as you work toward creating a consistent napping schedule. A more mature baby with a stabilized nap routine is easier to switch from the swing than an infant with a less predictable schedule.

Side by Side and Slip Away

Babies who sleep well when being held will often accept falling asleep by your side instead of in your arms. Babies who are breast-fed to sleep are perfect candidates for this approach to naptime settling. Like the previous idea, this can also be a midway point between in-arms naps and crib naps.

Create a baby-safe sleeping location that fits the two of you. A good choice is a mattress on the floor in your baby's room, which helps make a connection between his room and his naps. You can use an infant nest to create a smaller baby space on the mattress. Childproof the room and follow all standard co-sleeping safety guidelines (visit www.pantley.com/elizabeth).

Initiate a naptime routine: prepare your baby for sleep, darken the bedroom, turn on soft music or white noise, and lie down next to your baby on the mattress. You can place your hands on your baby or pat, rub, or nurse him to help settle him to sleep. As soon as he is asleep, slip quietly away. Keep your baby monitor turned on or stay close by so that you can return to your little one as soon as he is awake.

Create a Sibling Bed

If you have more than one child over a year old, consider creating a sleeping place where they can nap together. (Multiples or children close in age and size can be a bit younger if you follow co-sleeping safety rules.) Create a soothing prenap routine that includes reading to your children while they are in bed. Even if the youngest doesn't understand the story, your voice will be comforting, and this can become a beautiful family ritual.

Many parents report that co-sibling sleep is a wonderful way for children to bond their lifetime connection. We used the sibling bed idea in our family and found that our children truly enjoyed sleeping together. When my oldest daughter is home from college, you can occasionally find her snoozing with Coleton, our second grader. (Yes, naps are great for college kids, too!)

Duplicate Successful Bedtime Sleep

If your baby will nap only in your arms but goes to sleep easily in his bed at night, examine the differences between the two types of sleeping. Try to figure out how you can duplicate bedtime sleep for daytime naps.

One thing that often brings about better night sleep versus poor napping is that your baby is actually *tired* when bedtime arrives, but the nap schedule is off, and you're attempting to have him sleep when he's either not yet tired or overtired. Spend some time reviewing the sleep chart on page 8 and your baby's tired signs (pages 44 and 88) to bring you closer to the right nap schedule. The second cue that nighttime brings, which is lacking during the day, is the natural end of daytime light. To duplicate this, shut your baby's bedroom curtains and keep the room darker for naps.

The final factor that may be bringing you more success at night than during the day is your expectations and the actions that these bring. You *expect* your baby to sleep at night, and all your actions

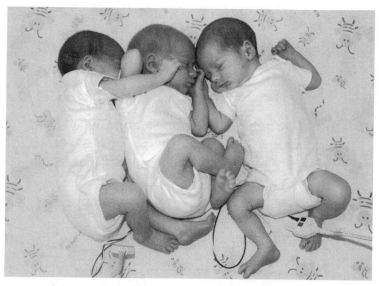

Angela, William, and John, triplets, fifteen days old

move him in that direction, whereas you may be viewing naps as optional. By understanding how important naps are and by acting more confidently about naptime, you can help your baby accept his daily naps. You might try "pretending" that it is bedtime when it's time for a nap, to create the same sequence of events that brings on night sleep. Treat lunch as if it is dinner, and then follow it up with a routine that is the same as bedtime. Often there are subtle differences that affect your baby's ability to fall asleep, and this false bedtime can uncover those differences. Once you have done this for a few days, you can modify the prenap routine so that it becomes a shorter, simpler version of the bedtime routine.

Naptime Nursling

Falling Asleep Without the Breast, Bottle, or Pacifier

....

See also: Changing from In-Arms Sleep to In-Bed Sleep;
Catnaps: Making Short Naps Longer; The Nap Resister:
When Your Child Needs a Nap but Won't Take One

> My son is ten months old. When he gets tired,
> I breastfeed him to sleep. If I try to put him
> down, he wakes up and grabs for me. This
> happens for every single nap. I love my son
> with all my heart, but I am starting to feel
> resentful and desperate. I have done this for ten
> months, and I simply cannot do it anymore!

As frustrating as this may be, it is normal behavior, and an exceptionally common nap problem. According to studies of naptime behaviors, 73 percent of breastfeeding babies fall asleep nursing, 67 percent of breastfeeding toddlers fall asleep nursing, and 33 percent of bottlefed children fall asleep while drinking from a bottle. This is no surprise; the most natural way for a baby to fall asleep is sucking while being held. It is a comforting ritual and a magic spell for sleep all rolled into one.

If your baby falls asleep nursing, drinking a bottle, or sucking on a pacifier and then you are able to put him into bed where he takes a nice, long nap, then nothing needs to change. There are parents who put their children down for a nap this way from birth through toddlerhood. So, if it works for you, consider yourself lucky that you have a wonderful way to help your child fall asleep. On the other hand, if you wish to change this pattern or if your child only catnaps once you put him in bed, you can use the ideas in this chapter to gently change your routine.

Most naptime nurslings are catnappers—they take short one-sleep-cycle naps of an hour or less. This is because when they shift from one sleep cycle to another, they have a brief awakening and become disoriented. They need to re-create the delightful sucking-to-sleep experience. If this describes your child, you can also read the chapter about catnappers on page 63. The combination of ideas from both chapters will work best to solve your napping problems.

The Grand Master of All Sleep Associations

Sucking is a powerful soothing mechanism for a baby. It activates the release of calming hormones in the nervous system which bring on relaxation, drowsiness, and ultimately, sleep. When coupled with the warm, snug, and safe place within a parent's arms, this is a potent and addictive sleep inducer. When a child *always* falls asleep this way, he associates these conditions with sleep, and over time he *cannot* fall asleep any other way, no matter how tired he may be.

In order to help a child switch from this naptime ceremony in a gentle way, you'll need to be patient and create new rituals. You'll most likely have the same routine for going to bed at night, so you'll have to work on bedtime, too. Some children can nurse to sleep at bedtime and then sleep through the night, even though they don't do so for naps. This is likely due to the powerful biological processes that make all human beings sleep at night. Naptime has a much more finicky biological response.

So, to begin, it's important to understand that your little one is being asked to give up something that he absolutely relies on for sleep. He isn't refusing a nap just to annoy you. Therefore, the best way to help him change this pattern is to gently provide him with new ways to fall asleep.

What About Pacifier Sucking?

New studies show that pacifier use for sleep may actually reduce the risk of SIDS, although it is unclear why the connection exists. At this time, professionals no longer discourage the use of pacifiers for falling asleep for babies up to one year of age, so if your baby benefits from having a pacifier for falling asleep, you can now rest assured that it is fine to use one.

I speculate that benefits also occur with nature's natural pacifier: mother's breast. That connection has not yet been identified in these studies, but it is something to watch for. Keep an eye on the work of researcher Dr. James J. McKenna, director of the Mother-Baby Behavioral Sleep Laboratory at the University of Notre Dame, who examines many of the benefits and aspects of breastfeeding and sleep.

The biggest issue for parents of a baby who uses a pacifier to fall asleep is that he wakes up when the pacifier falls out and won't go back to sleep until someone puts it back. The studies say that it is not necessary to replace a fallen pacifier, but these babies don't read studies—they just want their pacifier back in order to go back to sleep!

You can help your baby learn how to find and replace his own pacifier, if you wish. Simply guide his hand to it each time he awakens. To make it easier to locate a pacifier, put a few extra ones in the crib *after* he falls asleep. (Don't do this while he's awake or he'll come to depend on five pacifiers to fall asleep!) If you don't want your baby to become accustomed to sleeping with a pacifier, you can use the ideas that follow.

Sucking = Sleep

Many naptime nurslings do not have any wind-down period or prenap routine. They need no cue that it's time to sleep, and they require no sleep aid other than nursing or sucking their bottle or pacifier. It's a simple process: when they are ready to sleep, they suck and they are out! So, the sucking is actually the wind-down period, the routine, the sleep cue, the sleep aid, the lovey, and even the sleep place—all rolled into one.

In order to change this falling-asleep ritual, it helps to address all six components and create a nap schedule and routine that works with your child's biological sleep needs.

Create a Guideline Nap Schedule

Very often, naptime nurslings do not have a specific nap schedule. When they are fussy, they are breastfed or given a bottle or pacifier, and if the fussiness was caused by tiredness, they fall asleep. If you want to change the suck-to-sleep association, you'll need to start being more aware of your child's body clock as well as the kitchen clock. You'll need to begin to separate your child's need for sleep versus her need for comfort, nutrition, or company. By tuning into the different signals, you can more accurately pinpoint when her signs point to tiredness versus other needs.

A child who is put down for a nap at the correct biological moment will welcome sleep. The moment is perfect when she is just tired enough, but not overtired. This is the state when she is biologically prepped for sleep, so it is at this precise moment that she will be more likely to accept changes to her falling-asleep ritual.

The best way to determine your child's natural napping rhythm is to first—without changing your current routine—take a few days to learn the best sleep times. Start with a review of the sleep chart on page 8. Jot down the morning wake-up time and figure out the possible time span when a nap is likely. Beginning about a half hour before the earliest probable time, watch your child carefully for signs of tiredness. You can find a list of typical signs on pages 44 and 88. Keep in mind that every child is different, so it takes a bit of detective work to figure out the right signals. You may have been instinctually sensing them, so now it's time to accurately define them. Write down the times when tiredness appears and the times that he actually falls asleep.

> **Key Point**
>
> It's possible that up until now you've been following a child-led sleep routine, and the idea of setting up a nap schedule is foreign or uncomfortable. If you don't want to keep a log, calculate estimated sleep times, or set a schedule, you certainly don't have to do this. You can follow the other ideas in this section to make changes to your routine. However, having estimated sleep times will make naptime more predictable and therefore help everything else fall into place. Once your child is napping predictably and sleep issues are no longer a problem, then you can gradually return to a more flexible approach.

Wind-Down Period

It can be hard for a child to go directly from the action of the day to the quiet state necessary for sleep. Since nursing has been your child's method to wind down, you'll want to modify this so that he has an opportunity to calm and settle before sleep time. The best way to do this is to plan ahead. Once you have an approximate time for a nap, you can adjust your day to allow for a wind-down period.

Depending on the age and personality of your child, this could include quiet cuddle time in a darkened room, book reading, baby massage, or simply a reduction in the noise, light, and level of activity in the house.

Routine

It can help to create a short, specific prenap routine. It may be a good idea for this to be a mini-version of your bedtime routine, if you have one that helps him settle at night. Your routine is actually a series of subtle cues that signal that naptime is near. You'll want the routine to end up at the time that you feel your child is ready for sleep. Some of your wind-down activities can also be the start of your prenap routine.

An important key to a good nap routine is that it does not end with your child totally asleep at the breast, or with a bottle or pacifier, while in your arms. The last step of the routine should be your sleepy, relaxed little one in his bed. It's fine if you are there to pat or shush him, but if you want him to sleep in his bed, that's where he should land at the very end of your prenap routine. The routine not only acts as a cue (as described next), but it also activates a pattern to the day to help set your child's biological clock, which dictates when he will be tired.

Sleep Cue

There are a number of cues that you can use to tell your child that naptime is here. Moving to the darkened bedroom can be a strong cue. Quiet lullaby music, nature sound recordings, or white noise are also powerful signs that bring relaxation and tell your baby that it is bedtime. You can introduce certain fragrances to your naptime environment, such as vanilla or lavender, to further enhance the message that sleep time is here. If your baby is soothed by swaddling, this, too, is an important sleep cue. The final cue is your child's actual sleeping place: his bed.

Sleep Aids

Sleep aids are things that help your child to nod off to sleep. Of course the strongest sleep aid of any is nursing or sucking a bottle or pacifier, and one that you will continue to use, although in a slightly different way, which will be described in a minute. If your baby uses a pacifier, this is a good sleep aid. If your baby is over eighteen months old, a wonderful addition to the bed is a child-sized memory foam pillow—not for his head, but to be placed beside his hip or legs as something nice to lean against in bed.

Lovey

Many naptime nurslings have an attachment to the breast, bottle, or pacifier that goes beyond nutrition, sucking, and sleep to a deep emotional need. Your child might take to a transitional object, called a "lovey," for sleeping. These are usually stuffed animals or small baby-sized blankets. There are a wide variety of specially made loveys for infants. These are small, soft, and safe and can fulfill your child's need for naptime company.

To begin, include this lovey in your prenap and prebedtime routines. Keep it tucked between you so that it becomes a tactile and visual cue to sleep time. By tucking it between you, it also becomes warm and parent-scented, which makes it extra comforting. When you put your child in bed, tuck the lovey beside him.

Sleep Place

When your little nursling continues sucking until she is totally asleep, it is the last thing that she remembers. It is such a strong and overwhelming sensation that nothing else is acknowledged. This is why those who accept pacifiers will more often accept being placed into bed—because they can take their pacifier with them. (The trouble starts when the pacifier falls out!)

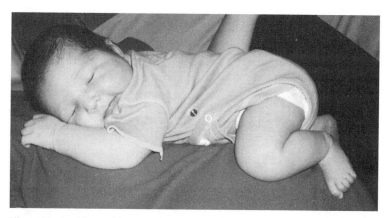

Kian, newborn, on Mommy Sacha

When you shift your child to her bed or if she has a brief awakening between sleep cycles and she finds the nipple missing, she will be shocked into wakefulness. You can help overcome this by creating a cozy, familiar nest for your child that woos her back to sleep when she starts to wake up.

One idea here is to arrange to spend some quiet playtime during the day in the place you want your child to nap. If this is his crib, lay him there and lean over toward him. Sing songs, talk, and point out the surroundings. Have two or three of these pleasant interludes during the day. If you can get your child interested in a toy or watching a mobile, then step away to the other side of the room for a minute, sit in a nearby chair, or even step out to the hallway and then return. By having these practice sessions, your child will come to know her crib as a welcoming and comfortable haven. It will become familiar, so she will then find comfort in falling asleep there or if she wakes mid-nap. This is effective for bedtime and night waking as well.

The other way to help your child accept the crib as his sleeping place is to be sure it is snug and inviting. You will find a list of ideas for making the crib cozy on page 140.

Mother-Speak

"As you suggested, we played with Dylan in his crib so he could get used to it. He has a mobile that he loves, and we let him 'play' with it two or three times a day. This has really helped him get used to his crib. I think that's one of the reasons he is starting to put himself back to sleep when he wakes up."

—Alison, mother of five-month-old Dylan

Your Newborn Nursling

Brand-new babies often fall asleep during nursing or while drinking a bottle. They "eat" first, and then they switch to nonnutritional pacifying as they drift off to sleep. When this happens consistently, they become accustomed to falling asleep with the sensation of the nipple in their mouth and then require this feeling not only to fall asleep but to fall *back to sleep* whenever they stir between sleep cycles. You can take a preventive measure with your newborn so that your baby doesn't become totally dependent on this type of sucking to be able to sleep. What you'll do, as often as you can, is remove the breast, bottle, or pacifier after your baby is finished drinking and let her finish falling asleep without having something in her mouth. This will give her an opportunity to fall asleep off the nipple.

 Pantley's Gentle Removal Plan

(Nicknamed by the No-Cry Sleep test moms as the "Pantley Pull-Off" or the "PPO")

If your baby or toddler always falls asleep nursing or sucking on a bottle or pacifier, it's likely that he relies on this sensation in order to fall asleep. Simply taking it away only creates a terrible amount of crying and pain (for parent and child). Pantley's Gentle Removal Plan is a step-by-step method to help your baby learn how to fall asleep without sucking.

A helpful first step is to create a phrase that signals, "We're all done now." You'll want to first use this at the end of each nursing or bottlefeeding session. As you finish, repeat your phrase two or three times. Choose your own phrase, based on your personality and your child's age, but it could be something like "All done. Milk is all done. Bye-bye milk." This becomes a "cue phrase" to close your nursing sessions and will be helpful when you would like your child to stop nursing and go to sleep.

When it's time for a nap, go ahead and nurse your child as you normally have. The difference is that instead of letting her *fall asleep* at the breast (or with a bottle), you will let her nurse for feeding, until her sucking slows and she is relaxed and sleepy. Make sure your child is done "drinking" and just pacifying, which is often characterized with a fluttery on/off pattern of sucking. Then you'll want to take your nursling off the breast or remove the bottle or pacifier. There are several ways to do this.

- You can break the seal with your finger and gently remove the nipple from her mouth.
- You can use a quicker, more confident break with your finger. If you are sitting, you might want to immediately move her up to your shoulder and hold her snugly while you swing/sway/swish/pat/shush or otherwise comfort her.
- If you are lying beside her, use the quick, confident release, and then shift your breasts away from her face (perhaps turn on your tummy somewhat) or hide the bottle from sight while patting, rubbing, rocking, or whatever soothes her.

Continued

Don't use your closing phrase just yet! At first, your child will be confused and want to continue nursing—because that's what she has always done. You may be able to very gently hold her mouth closed with mild pressure or a gentle massage under her chin or just under her lip (this helps to ease her mouth from sucking to stillness); at the same time rock or sway with her, and say, "Shhh. Shhh." If she struggles or fusses, go ahead and let her nurse a bit more since you don't want her to become totally awake and start crying, but repeat the removal process every few minutes until she finally falls asleep.

How long between removals? Every child is different, but about ten to thirty seconds between removals usually works. You can count to thirty if that helps you relax and stay on task. (You'll not want to remove in the middle of a let-down unless you're prepared to hold your hand over your breast to stop the milk flow.)

It may take two, three, five, or even more attempts, but eventually your child will accept the loss of the nipple, get comfortable, and begin to fall asleep without the nipple in his mouth. *This* is when you can say your closing phrase—very quietly! You are creating a connection between the closing phrase and her actually being *finished* nursing.

When you've done this a number of times, over a period of days, you should find that the removals are much easier. This is when you will begin to use your closing phrase earlier in the process and begin to be more persistent in ending the nursing session earlier. As the Gentle Removal begins to work, it's important to pull off sooner and sooner in the process. (If you don't shorten the time, your nursling will just become used to a long, drawn-out removal process.) When the removal is shortened a little at a time, one day your child will surprise you by pulling off on her own. But to get there you must have consistency on your part.

Mother-Speak

"We call this our Big PPO (Pantley Pull-Off). At first Joshua would see it coming and grab my nipple tighter in anticipation—ouch! But you said to stick with it, and I did. Now he anticipates the PPO and actually lets go and turns and rolls over on his side to go to sleep! I am truly amazed."

—**Shannon, mother of nineteen-month-old Joshua**

Repeat the gentle removal process at every nap, and also every night if your child nurses to sleep at bedtime or during night waking, until your little one learns that she can fall asleep without nursing.

Patience with Your Child, Patience with Yourself

At any time if you feel too frustrated to continue with the "PPO," just let your little one nurse to sleep, and try again at the next nap. Don't feel you must succeed quickly. This process may take some time. Be patient. There are no awards for being the first parent on your block to have your child fall asleep without your help!

Remember, too, that all the solutions in this book can work together like pieces to a big sleep puzzle. Make sure that you are applying all the other information you've learned about your child's sleep in other parts of this book. If your sleep plan is a complete one, you will see your child's daily naps improving more quickly.

Swinging, Bouncing, Vibrating, or Gliding

Making the Transition from Motion Sleep to Stationary Sleep

....

See also: Changing from In-Arms Sleep to In-Bed Sleep; The Nap Resister: When Your Child Needs a Nap but Won't Take One

> My six-week-old son is a terrible napper. As a newborn he would only sleep while being held. I once put him in the crib, but he cried until he fell asleep and then only napped for fifteen minutes. I refuse to do that again! I discovered that he will take a nice, long nap when I put him in his swing, so that's what we do. I have been told that sleep tainted by movement is poor sleep and harmful for my baby. Is this true? How will I get him to sleep in a motionless bed without making him cry?

Let's think back. Prior to six weeks ago, how did your baby sleep? He slept in a fluid bed that sloshed and moved with your every step. You walked, bounced up stairs, and may have even jogged or taken an aerobics class! And if you loved your rocking chair—imagine that! That is *not* what I would call motionless sleep! Right now I would like you to get up, put both hands firmly on your belly, and walk around the house, go up and down the stairs, bend up and down as if folding laundry or loading dishes, and jog in place. This was how your baby slept—up to *twenty hours* each and every day before birth. Can you now understand why an unmoving, flat crib can be unsettling to your new baby?

Your baby didn't magically transform into a different life form at the moment of birth; he was the same person he was just a minute before. That's the reason that the first three months of life are often referred to as the "fourth trimester." There is a time of transition from womb to world that takes months, usually even lingering long past this fourth trimester. After this transition time, the comforts of motion sleep become a happy habit. But harmful? Ask any adult who loves rocking chairs, gliders, hammocks, or sleeping on the train. They will tell you that motion can be comforting and restful.

Human beings have been rocking babies to sleep for as long as there have been babies. It's a very natural way to help them sleep. Parents instinctually search for ways to provide their babies with movement to settle them because it works so well. There are a number of interesting methods that parents use: bouncing on an exercise ball, dancing or swaying in a sling, driving in a car, and even holding an infant chair on top of the washing machine. (If your baby enjoys movement *and* being held in your arms, you will find ideas in this chapter as well as the chapter "Changing from In-Arms Sleep to In-Bed Sleep.")

Why Babies Sleep Well with Motion

Babies often nap better when we try to re-create the experiences from the womb. This explains why babies enjoy a sleeping place that is warm, closely held, slightly noisy, and gently moving. Being held in a parent's arms creates the perfect combination of these things, but a busy parent cannot possibly hold a napping baby for hours every day. The next best solution is a swing, glider, hammock, rocking cradle, or vibrating infant seat. Motion naps in these devices are incredibly popular with babies since they mimic the experience of the *womb* environment in four ways:

- **W—Whooshing sounds:** The pleasant swooshing white noise sounds of the motor and the creaking of the swing are similar to the sounds of the heartbeat and fluids heard in the womb. Not only do they soothe your baby to sleep, they also block out outside noises that interfere with a nap. They are a powerful sleep cue that says *time to nap.*

- **O—Orderly, predictable events:** Diaper changed, child into the seat, buckle clicked, music on, swaying begins, sleep time! It's exactly the same every single time—very predictable and a memorable routine.

- **M—Movement:** The gentle, consistent sway creates a pleasant rocking that mimics the sway and movement of the womb. This rocking is the same instinctual movement you use when you settle your baby in your arms.

- **B—Buckled:** Snug in her seat, your baby's own movements don't startle her awake. In addition, she isn't free to move around, play, explore, and thus evade sleep. She's cradled in a cozy space, much like being encased in the womb.

Those four components together create a sleep-inducing environment for a baby—they soothe him and help him relax and fall asleep. Additionally, every time a baby shifts between sleep cycles or if noises wake him up, these components can lull him back to sleep before he fully wakes, resulting in a nice, long nap.

We often add a fifth item to this list without even realizing it. The swing or bouncer is usually in the main part of the house near *people,* and the crib is off in a room by itself. Since babies are naturally drawn to being with the people they love, the infant seat or swing has another advantage over the crib. Your presence and the quiet voices and noises of the household can be a soothing addition to your baby's nap environment.

Babies who suffer from colic, reflux, colds, or other medical ailments can benefit from yet another feature: the slight incline of the cradle, which can alleviate some of their discomfort. Babies with special needs and sensory integration issues can often benefit from daily naps in a swing, rocker, hammock, or bouncer—ask your medical care professional for more information.

Professional-Speak

"Throughout time, parents have had kith and kin to lend hands of support. In today's mini-families, a swing or a sling can help replace that missing extra pair of hands you need to comfort your baby."

—**Harvey Karp, M.D., author and creator of the book, CD, and DVD** *The Happiest Baby on the Block*

The Negative Aspects of Motion Naps

As it seems is always the case in parenting, no matter how great something seems, there always has to be another side of the story. Motion naps are not perfect; they do have their bad side. Here are the potential problems and a few tips to overcome them:

- If your baby gets accustomed to napping in his swing, glider, or infant seat, then you may be forced to either stay home at all naptimes or deal with an overtired, cranky baby. The good news is that most often babies who sleep in these devices will also sleep well in a stroller or in your arms. So, if you are willing to hold your napping baby in a restaurant, at a movie, or at a friend's home, then you've solved the majority of issues related to this potential problem.

- Convincing your baby to nap while traveling can be complicated if you can't bring the swing or seat with you on your trip.

There is a possibility that you can borrow or rent a swing. Check with rental companies that rent lawn and garden equipment and party supplies; they often have baby swings. A travel-size swing, cradle, or small bouncer or vibrating seat is a good option to take along with you on a trip. You can also bring along a folding stroller that can even be used indoors. Or bring an easy-to-pack sling and carry your baby for naps. (For more tips on travel, see page 223.)

• You'll have to make a change to a stationary bed at some point. All swings, seats, and gliders have size and weight limits, and for good reasons. A baby who is too big can cause the apparatus to tip over. A baby who is too old might roll or climb out, or reach out to pull down an attachment or connection. Very often by the time babies outgrow their swings, they are developmentally

Daddy Matthew Sr. and Alyssa Maria, five months old

ready to move to a stationary bed for their naps. Further in this chapter you'll find many ideas for making the change once you are ready.

• If your baby is content in his swing, there is the risk that you'll overuse the device. Even if you believe that excess use of baby holders is not in your child's best interest, overuse can sneak up on you. One of the ways to avoid being drawn into the overuse of baby holders is to decide that you'll use them *only* for naptime and avoid having your baby in the seat when he is awake. That's the time for parent-baby interaction.

Protecting That Sweet Little Head

When your baby sleeps in a seat of any kind, he will have little ability to move his head in different positions. If your baby also spends awake hours in seats (swings, bouncers, car seats) or even lying on his back in a crib, he may be at risk for developing a flat area on the back of his head (called *positional plagiocephaly* or *flathead syndrome*). By being aware of this, you can take steps to protect your baby. There are several ways to avoid positional plagiocephaly.

- Reduce the number of hours your baby spends in reclined seats of any kind or lying on his back during *waking hours*.
- When you put your baby down to sleep, vary the position of his head; slightly turn his head to the left, right, or center instead of always laying him nose up.
- Move the location of the seat every day or two so that the things your baby sees before she falls asleep and when she wakes up are on the opposite sides of her.
- Be certain that your baby has plenty of time every day being held upright, since when you carry your baby, there is no pressure on the back part of the skull. Being held also strengthens your baby's muscles, preparing him to hold himself upright.

- Make sure that your baby has lots of tummy time for play during the day. This not only avoids pressure on the back of the head, but it also help your baby develop his neck and back muscles.
- Vary the locations of your baby's toys and mobiles so that your baby isn't always looking the same direction.
- Alternate the direction of your baby when you change diapers, feed, carry, or play.
- Put a folded baby washcloth under the padding of the swing on alternating sides of your baby's headrest or under his shoulder to slightly change the angle of pressure on your baby's head. Switch the position every day or two.
- Alternate your baby's position from one side to the other when holding, breastfeeding, or bottlefeeding.

Safe Sleeping in a Swing, Bouncer, or Glider

If you choose to have your baby take naps in a swing, bouncy seat, or glider, there are some important safety factors for you to be aware of. Keep the following information in mind:

- For naps, use a cradle-style bed in lieu of an upright chair-style seat. You want your baby lying as close to the same position she would in a crib as possible: flat on her back. Daily naps in the seated position can negatively affect development of the back, hips, and legs. A baby who sleeps in a seated position can slump over, and this can hinder his breathing. Adjust the seat to tilt back as much as possible, and use a cushioned head support to prevent slumping.
- Keep your baby near you or invest in a quality baby monitor and check on your baby frequently. Safety experts recommend that you not leave your baby alone if he is sleeping in a swing or infant seat unless it is specifically made for solitary sleep.
- Use the slowest, gentlest speed that settles your baby. If your baby requires a high speed to be able to fall asleep, you can work toward slowing this down over a period of time. When you make

changes by small increments, it's likely your baby will accept the change, particularly if all other parts of his routine remain the same.

• Turn the swing or vibration off or to its lowest setting once your baby is asleep so that she isn't swinging or vibrating at high speed for the entire nap. Turn the swing back on if your baby begins to wake up before an appropriate length of naptime. If he's between sleep cycles, this will help him fall back to sleep.

• Always use the safety harness and straps properly, according to the directions provided with the product.

• Never place a swing or seat on a table, counter, or other elevated surface.

• Never leave a baby alone with a dog or a toddler. The dog might "chase" the moving swing or try to play with the baby or the toys. A protective dog might respond and "help" the baby if he cries. A toddler might attempt to play with the baby or help him and wake him up or, worse, accidentally knock the swing over.

• Read and follow the instructions and safety information that comes with the product, including weight limitations.

Mother-Speak

"My daughter had colic. I tried everything under the sun to get her to nap in the afternoon, but all she did was cry. Even carrying her in my arms didn't work—I would walk with her for hours, and she never stopped crying. This made me feel drained and helpless. I discovered that when I swaddled her and put her in the swing she would fall asleep easily and sleep for two hours. There was absolutely no way I would have been able to survive colic without the swing. I am slowly weaning her now, and it is taking a lot of patience. But those months of peace were definitely worth it for both of us."

—Natalia, mother of seven-month-old Eva

Buying the Right Product

When shopping for a swing, hammock, or bouncy seat, take plenty of time to choose the right product. If possible, bring your baby along and experiment with the floor model. He may not take to it immediately (especially in the store environment), but it will give you an idea of how he fits and how easy it is to use. Take time to compare options and consider these points:

- Purchase only a new product, as safety features are improved constantly. Older, used swings, bouncers, and seats may not be safe for your sleeping baby.
- Check to be sure there is a stable base and sturdy construction.
- Look for a certification from the Juvenile Products Manufacturers Association or other formal safety organization.
- Consider neutral colors and fewer frills, since bright colors and attachments can be interesting for a playful baby but distracting if your baby is trying to sleep.
- Choose a product that has soft lullaby music, white noise, nature sounds, or no sounds at all. Whether a swing has built-in sound is a minor consideration, though, since you can use another source for this.
- Pick a swing or chair with an accessible seat that allows you easy-in, easy-out access, especially for a sleeping baby.
- Choose a cozy, cradle-style seat for comfortable sleeping, sized for your baby now and months from now, if possible. Read the package for size and weight restrictions.
- Listen for a pleasant sound while the motor is running. Listen for one that will be soothing to your baby and to you.
- Pick a product with a volume button for the music or sounds, *plus* an on/off button to turn off the sounds independently of the motion, so you can have your baby swing without the sound.

- Shop for a product with a secure five-point harness system that will keep your baby safe from becoming entangled or slipping out of the swing.
- Choose a model with variable speeds and possibly several swinging directions so that you can adjust it to suit your baby.
- If possible, choose a model with a timer that can turn the swing or vibration off after your baby is sleeping.
- Pick a model with a removable toy bar that can be taken off for naptime, as these can be distracting if you want your baby to sleep.
- Look for a model with a removable, machine-washable cover.
- Find out if the motor needs to be plugged in or runs by batteries. If battery-operated, have a supply of batteries on hand or consider two sets of rechargeable batteries.
- If you don't have a swing, bouncer, or hammock now but are looking to buy one, you might consider borrowing one, renting one, or letting your baby take a test ride in a friend's swing. Babies don't always take to these immediately, but you might get a sense if this will work for your child.

Father-Speak

"My son sleeps so well in the swing that I use it every day. While he swings, I make phone calls and do other things I can't do when he's awake. When he wakes up, we play. After listening to other parents complain about their non-napping babies, I got to feeling guilty about how easy it is for us: swaddle, swing, snooze. But then I had an epiphany. He's happy and healthy, and we both benefit from his naps, so why not?"

—Jay, father to four-month-old Maxwell

The Sensible Use of Swings and Things

A parent should never be made to feel guilty for using a swing to help a baby achieve a long, wonderful nap. But let's never be tempted to allow these devices to take the place of our loving arms. That's the first place of choice for all babies!

How to Decide When to Wean Your Baby from Motion Naps

There is no absolute rule for when you must wean your baby from motion naps to stationary sleep. The right decision is different for every child. The following questions can guide you as you determine if you should continue naps as they are or if it is the right time to move your child to stationary sleep:

- How do your child's daily nap hours match up to the sleep chart on page 8? Is she getting enough sleep and napping often enough throughout the day?
- Is your baby safe? Has he outgrown the seat?
- Is everyone in the family happy with the way things are going now?
- Is the motion sleep becoming troublesome or complicated? Why?

Understand the Elements of Your Baby's Motion Sleep

Once you have decided that it is time to transition your baby to stationary sleep, take a day or two to analyze your baby's current routine. Once you understand the schedule as it is now, you can decide what you would prefer it to be and then make a plan for changes.

Be patient, as the transformation could take anywhere from a week to several months, depending on how deeply ingrained the

Kieran, three years old, and Mommy Jennifer

motion habit is, the actual reasons your baby is attached to motion naps, how well the solutions you pick match your baby's personality, and how dedicated you are to make the change happen. It's important to decide up front if you want to make the change as quickly as possible or if you would rather take time to allow the change to be more gradual.

Before you move on to choosing solutions, let's look at the components to your child's current nap environment so that you address each of them:

- **Movement.** (Obviously!) But what speed? What direction? Is it used to help him get drowsy, to fall asleep, to stay asleep, or all three of these?
- **Sound.** What music or sounds does your baby hear as she is falling asleep? During sleep? (Beyond the music, listen for motor

hum, creaking, and other sounds.) What other sounds does your baby hear during naps? (Kitchen noises, laundry room sounds, sibling voices?)

- **Structure of the sleeping surface.** What shape? What texture? How soft or firm? Does your baby have contact on one, two, or three sides of her body? How is she kept warm—clothing, blanket?
- **Location.** Where does your baby take naps now? Where are you while he is napping? What can your baby see from his sleeping place? How light is the room?
- **Routine.** Babies who take motion naps often require no routine at all! Just pop baby in the swing, turn it on, and it's off to visit the sandman. Consider what happens the half hour before nap: feeding, diaper change, and anything else that routinely occurs before sleep. These components can be used in your new stationary-sleep routine.

How to Transition Your Baby to Stationary Sleep

All babies are different, so there isn't one perfect solution that fits all. Here is an assortment of ideas for you to choose from, combine, or perhaps use as inspiration to come up with your own best answer.

Step-by-Step

Instead of changing everything about your baby's nap all at once, it may help to make the switch in stages. Here is one example to give you an idea of how this works—your step-by-step may be entirely different. The steps you create are not set in stone. You might need to adjust the plan as you go along. At each stage listed, all the routine steps remain exactly the same except for the one change noted. (Again, this is a sample and can be modified as suits you and your baby.) The steps planned are these:

- If you do not use white noise for naptime now, begin to use it for naptime. Select a soothing sound such as ocean waves, heart sounds, or rainfall. (Look for a CD or a white-noise device; don't use the sound that comes attached to the swing.) Use this for a week or so in your baby's current location, as it will become a consistent sleep cue through all the remaining steps.
- Set up the swing in the baby's bedroom right beside the crib. Do nothing else different (except play your new sounds) for a week so your baby can get used to the new location. (If baby doesn't settle easily, then sit with him in the room. Read, fold laundry, or do yoga so that your relaxed presence tells him everything is okay.)
- Begin to use a slower speed on the swing.
- After a time, shut the movement off as soon as baby is asleep.
- Once this adjustment is made, try putting baby in the swing for naps but turn the movement off when baby is settled and sleepy, before he is actually asleep.
- Next, follow all your usual routine, but do *not* turn the movement on at all.
- After a week or so of your baby sleeping in the stationary swing, put him down for a nap in the crib. Prepare the crib in advance to make it more inviting, as described on page 140. Incorporate other ideas as shown in the following sections.

Step-by-Step, with a Twist

Some babies are so accustomed to motion during their naps that they won't take to the idea of sleeping stationary—even in their familiar swing. You may have tried to shut off the motion, but your baby just cries and won't nap, making it hopeless to even think your baby would nap in the crib. There are a few creative ways to bring motion to the crib. In most cases it's still helpful to follow the step-by-step idea previously described, but when it's time to put your baby into the crib, that's where you make one adjustment: add some movement. Here are a few ways to do this:

• **Mimic the motion.** Take a small handheld massaging vibration device (used for back rubs) and turn it on. Place it in the corner of the crib (away from your baby) and put your sleeping or drowsy baby down in the crib. The feel of the vibration and the sound can help your baby fall asleep and stay asleep. You must keep an eye on your baby or remove the massager from the crib once your baby is sleeping.

• **Use a bouncy chair or vibrating seat.** Take a bouncy or vibrating seat and put it *in the crib.* Make sure that the seat is stable so that it won't tip over. To keep your baby safe, you must stay in the room or sit in a chair in the doorway so you can keep an eye on your baby. Turn the vibration off after your baby falls asleep so that he'll be more used to sleeping stationary in the crib. After a time of using the seat in this way, gradually reduce the speed of the vibration until you finally turn it off completely. The next step is to keep the nap routine exactly the same but remove the seat and lay your baby directly in the crib. When you first do this, your baby might be confused, so when you place him in bed, lay your hands on him and rub or pat to help him get settled.

• **Attach a crib-vibrating device.** There are a few crib-vibrating devices on the market that attach to the bottom springs below the mattress. Some of these also have a white noise attachment. While no studies have been done to prove their effectiveness, some parents swear by them. Most of these have a return policy in case you find it doesn't work for you. As an alternative, you may be able to remove the vibrating box from an outgrown bouncy seat for this purpose and tape it to the bottom of the crib. (This is especially effective if it is one that your baby loved when she was younger.)

Duplicate the Familiar Parts of the Sleep Environment

One way to make the crib more agreeable is to mimic parts of your baby's current swing or napping seat. Here are a few ideas:

- Is there a headrest pad in your baby's swing that you can transfer to the crib? A head support made for strollers can work, also. (This idea is not for newborns—safety dictates no pillows for infants.) An infant positioner can also create that cradled feeling for your baby.
- Can you put the swing in the room *next to the crib* and turn it on while your baby is in the crib? The familiar sound— even when your baby is not in the swing—may be comforting and can be a good sleep cue.
- Can you place a crib wedge under the bedding to create a slightly upright angle that is more similar to his swing angle?
- Is there a safety bar that goes between your child's legs in his seat? You can place a small, safe stuffed animal between his legs in the crib to replicate that feeling.
- The swing-bed is likely small so your baby can touch the sides. Instead of laying her in the middle of the crib, try positioning her at the top or bottom corner. That way she can feel the sides of the crib near her.
- Put a stationary cradle in the place where the swing usually sits so the surroundings are familiar.

Experiment with Baby Massage

Babies who are accustomed to the multisensory stimulation provided by motion naps may find a prenap massage relaxing enough to prepare them for sleep. Massage for this purpose is best done after a diaper change in a darkened room, preferably the same room where your baby will nap. Peaceful music or white noise plus a bit of lavender fragrance can further create a relaxing ambience for your little one.

Create a calming routine for your baby and follow it exactly for a week or so to see how effective it will be. Choose a week when disruptions are minimal and you can be home every day at naptime. Start your new routine about a half hour before your baby's typical nap time. If he has no typical time, watch his behavior for tired signs.

Jot down your new routine (see page 29) and follow it step-by-step. It might include a bath if that relaxes your baby, and if you start the routine *before* your baby is showing signs of tiredness, so you'll have plenty of time. Move to a quiet, darkened room. Turn on soft music or white noise and give your baby a massage. At the end of the massage, simply lay your hands on your baby for a few minutes to see if she is drowsy enough to sleep. She should be relaxed and peaceful.

If you are unfamiliar with how baby massage works, ask your health care provider, midwife, doula, or lactation consultant for guidance. Or check out one of the many wonderful classes or books on baby massage.

Move Your Sleeping Baby

If your baby will not fall asleep in the crib but falls deeply asleep in the swing, try letting her fall asleep in the swing and then move her while she sleeps. Set up her bedroom to be inviting for sleep: pull down the shades, turn on soft music or white noise, and warm up the sheets with a heat pack or warm towel (remove these before you lay your baby down). It can help to locate the swing in the bedroom next to the crib so that you aren't traveling a long distance between the two places.

As soon as she is asleep, carefully transfer her to the bed. Make your movements slow but steady. You might also try the Pantley Dance, as described starting on page 144.

If your baby wakes the minute she touches the crib, try putting a travel cradle or Moses basket in the crib to make it a smaller space, or add a soft mattress pad under flannel sheets. For more ideas on how to make the crib cozy, see page 140.

Key Point

Any time you change what you are doing at naptime, your baby may resist the idea. Stay with any new idea for a few weeks to allow your baby to adjust before you judge its true effectiveness.

Night Sleep in the Crib, but Day Sleep in a Swing?

A surprising number of parents report that their baby sleeps fine at night in the crib, cradle, or bed but won't nap there during the day. For daytime naps they must turn to motion sleep. There are three main reasons this happens: your night routine is more specific than your nap routine, you are misreading your baby's tired signs and attempting naps at times when your baby is not sleepy or is extremely overtired, or you co-sleep with your baby, which is an acceptable alternative for most children.

If your baby takes to the crib at night but not for naps, the first step is to take a look at your successful bedtime routine and re-create it for naptime. You may not realize the many subtle differences between the two until you act them out. The easiest way to do this is to simply fool yourself and your baby into thinking it is bedtime. Do exactly what you do in the evening—even though it's really noon!

The second thing to watch is the span of wakeful time between sleep sessions. Be sure your baby has been awake long enough, yet not too long, by naptime. Check the chart on page 8 and also watch your baby for some of the tired signs listed on pages 44 and 88.

Keep Trying!

If your baby totally resists all attempts you make to have her nap in her crib, then sometimes it's best to leave well enough alone for a week or two or even longer. Then try again, perhaps with a different plan. Sometimes a slight change to your approach along with a few weeks of maturity can make a big difference in the end result. All babies eventually outgrow the need for motion during naptime.

Helping Your Newborn Tummy Sleeper Go "Back to Sleep"

> **I know that my newborn should sleep on her back, but she hates it! When I let her sleep on her tummy, she naps longer and better, so I'm tempted to let her sleep that way. Would that be a good idea?**

When you've found a way to help your baby sleep better, it is tempting to give in, no matter what. However, when your baby's safety is at risk, it's not worth the few hours of sleep you'll gain. Studies have proved scientifically that back sleeping is the safest way for babies to sleep, due to the higher risk of sudden infant death syndrome (SIDS) when stomach sleeping. SIDS is not totally preventable, nor can it be diagnosed before it occurs, but this is one factor that parents can control. In most cases, infants who sleep on their backs are less susceptible to SIDS than those who sleep on their stomachs.

This isn't an issue you'll need to deal with forever, as your baby will (far too soon) grow out of the newborn stage. There isn't an exact age when belly sleeping becomes a safe position; this is unique to every child. However, most specialists imply that once your baby can hold her head up steadily and roll easily from belly to back and back to belly, you can put her to sleep on her back and then let her find her own comfortable position.

Once your doctor confirms that back sleeping is best for your baby, always put her to sleep on her back. If your little one resists this sleep position, try the following ideas to encourage back sleeping.

Investigate Using an Infant Sleep-Positioning System

There are a wide variety of infant sleep-positioning systems on the market. These are often made of foam and have two side bolsters (round or triangular) connected by a bottom piece of fabric. At this time, none of these carry a recommendation or stamp of approval by any medical group, as more research needs to be completed on the safety of these products. Nonetheless, they are becoming very popular and are even recommended by some pediatricians. The designs are constantly improving, so search around for the best one you can find.

Many parents use positioners successfully for babies who resist back sleeping or who have reflux or other digestive problems. Many say that when they firmly swaddle their baby and place him on his back in a properly fitting positioner, it solves many sleep problems. Ask around and search the Internet for parent recommendations on these, and talk with your medical professional about using one for your baby.

When your baby can roll from back to front and front to back, it's time to stop using a positioner. If your baby rebels at first, you can remove one side of the positioner. Also, increase the number of tummy-time floor-practice sessions throughout each day to help your baby practice this new rolling skill. Within a few weeks, your baby will have mastered this maneuver and will be more comfortable in his crib.

Use a Crib Alternative for Naps

Sleeping in a sling, stroller, swing, or infant seat will keep your baby slightly curled, rather than flat on a mattress. Many tummy sleepers enjoy the curved position much more than lying flat on their backs. In addition, these carriers have a more flexible, softer surface that invites sleep. Be sure to follow safety precautions and

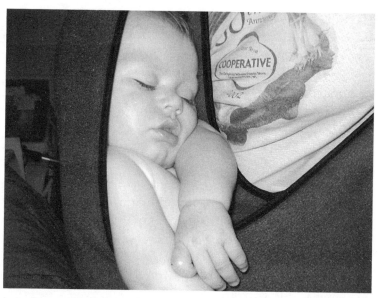

Luca Eamon, seven months old, in Mama's sling

read the instructions that come with the device. Manufacturers of car seats, strollers, and infant seats warn parents not to leave a baby alone in these seats, so this idea works only when you are awake and close by for naps; they aren't good places for night sleep. Keep an eye on your baby and watch to be sure he doesn't twist around in the seat, become entangled in the straps, or hunch too far forward, as this can interfere with proper breathing.

While a car seat creates a nice nest for sleeping, new studies tell us that babies should not be left to sleep for long spans in a car seat because the positioning can also interfere with proper breathing. There are a number of positioning cushions that can be used in a car seat or baby seat to hold your baby's upper body in a safer sleep position. These typically have a pad that is placed under the baby's back with side "wings" to prevent a baby's head from wobbling. New designs of some car seats allow them to adjust to lie flat when taken out of the car. If your baby often falls asleep in the car seat, it would be worth it to check out a seat of this style.

While all of these alternative places may help your baby nap better, there will soon come a time when you would like the freedom of putting your baby down for a nap in a bed and taking some baby-free time while he sleeps. Even though you'll likely have to help your baby adjust to the change at some point, the vast majority of parents feel it is still worth it to use these nestlike places to improve their newborn's sleep.

When it's time to help your baby make the transition to a flat crib, try moving him after he is asleep. Or you can pat or rub your baby's tummy, legs, or head at the transition to be sure he stays asleep. Or use the Pantley Dance transfer method described on page 144. You can also put him in a rocking cradle, which makes up for the flat surface with gentle movement. For more ideas on weaning to a crib for naps, see the chapter "Swinging, Bouncing, Vibrating, or Gliding: Making the Transition from Motion Sleep to Stationary Sleep."

Use a Baby Hammock

Babies who resist lying on their backs on a traditional mattress will often welcome back sleeping in a baby hammock. These safely cradle your baby in a comforting fetal position. Hammocks provide a more flexible, yielding surface and provide soothing sleep-inducing movement, as well. A baby hammock is especially helpful if your baby is a preemie, a restless sleeper, or a short napper or if he has colic, reflux, allergies, or any other health issues. Shop around to find a model that suits you and your baby.

Try Swaddling Your Baby for Naps

Very often a baby who resists sleeping on her back finds the position difficult because of her natural startle reflexes. When her arms or legs move in ways that she can't easily control, this prevents her from sleeping or startles her awake. Being swaddled prevents her natural reflexes from waking her up. (For more about swaddling, see the chapter "How to Use Swaddling for Naptime.")

Warm Up Your Baby's Sleeping Surface

Some babies may not actually object to back sleeping but to the transition from your warm arms to a cold bed. You can place a heating pad set on the lowest setting or a bead-filled warmer on your baby's mattress just before naptime. Remove the heat source and rub your arm over the surface to be sure it is not too hot for your baby, and then lay your baby down on the nice, warm bed. Keep your hand on your baby's tummy for a minute or two and then slowly move your hand away. This gradual transition can help your baby accept his bed for naptime.

Wait Until Your Baby Is Sleeping and Gently Turn Him Over

If your baby truly resists back sleeping yet you know that he is overtired and needing a nap, you can stay with him while he falls asleep on his tummy, and when he is asleep, gently turn him over. This isn't the best overall solution, since you don't want to have to be involved in your baby's every nap or run the risk of leaving him to sleep on his tummy. You also don't want to encourage tummy sleeping. However, when your baby is overtired, this can be a help-ful temporary solution.

Monitor Your Baby's Health

A baby who is suffering from reflux, an ear infection, or other health problem might be resisting sleep for this reason. If your baby seems physically uncomfortable with back sleeping, talk it over with your health care provider.

Talk to Your Doctor About a Compromise: Side Sleeping

In most cases, side sleeping is a very distant second choice to back sleeping, but if your baby absolutely will not sleep on his back, you can discuss this option with your health care provider. Ask if a specialty sleeping wedge or tightly rolled baby blanket can be used to hold your baby in this position.

Provide Lots and Lots *and Lots* of Daytime Tummy Playtime

Tummy sleeping becomes safe when your baby is able to have full control of her head, arms, and body, moving freely from tummy to side to back. To encourage this development, give your baby plenty of floor time to develop her muscle control.

Create a safe place on the floor with a clean mat. Surround your baby with toys. And get down there with him! Nothing will motivate your baby more than a loving playmate.

Keep Your Baby's Bed Safe

Finally, if you still choose to have your baby sleep on her tummy despite everything you've read, heard, and been told—or if your doctor has approved this position—make certain that your baby's mattress is even, firm, and flat. Every time you put her to bed, check to be sure that the sheets are clean, smooth, and tightly secured. Don't put any pillows, blankets, or toys in bed with her. Remove bumper pads, and be sure your mattress fits properly in the crib. If you have concerns, ask your doctor or hospital about renting a sophisticated device that monitors baby's sound, movement, and breathing. (These should never be used without a doctor's supervision.)

Now That Your Baby Is Sleeping on Her Back

Congratulations! Your baby is now an official back sleeper. As soon as your baby gains control of her body movements and is able to hold her head up and master rolling back and forth on her own, she'll be free to sleep in whatever position she finds most comfortable. In the meantime, look over the pointers on page 171 to protect your baby's head from developing a flat spot, a potential but avoidable side effect caused by back sleeping.

Back Sleeping at Day Care or with Babysitters

If your baby naps while under the care of a babysitter, relative, or day care provider, you'll want to discuss back sleeping with these adults. Not all child care centers have policies on infant sleep positions; or even when they do, not all child care providers abide by the guidelines. Babies who are not used to sleeping on their stomachs are at a particularly high risk for SIDS when placed in this position at day care. Check on the policies in your center, and be sure that they are placing your baby in the proper sleep position as recommended by specialists and your doctor.

This Phase Passes Quickly

Even if your newborn never adjusts happily to back sleeping, you can take heart in knowing that this is a temporary issue. In a few weeks when your baby is able to better control his body, he'll be safe sleeping in whatever position he desires.

How to Use Swaddling for Naptime

....

See also: The Nap Resister: When Your Child Needs a Nap but Won't Take One; Swinging, Bouncing, Vibrating, or Gliding: Making the Transition from Motion Sleep to Stationary Sleep

My newborn was swaddled at the hospital. Now that we're home, should we continue to swaddle her? When should we wean her from it and how?

Swaddling your baby is a fantastic way to calm her and help her to nap better and longer because it creates a womblike feeling: she's snugly tucked in and warmly embraced on all sides. In addition, since your baby's arms and legs are tucked tightly, this can prevent the startle reflex from waking her up from her nap before she's ready to be awake. Swaddling can be especially helpful as a nap aid if your baby is colicky or fussy.

How to Swaddle Your Baby

If you're new to swaddling, it can be a bit confusing. However, when you've done it a few times, it will become effortless. Your baby might also require a little bit of time to adjust to swaddling, so allow him a few practice times before you decide if this is a good choice for your infant's naptime.

You'll need a blanket that's not too much bigger than your newborn—a square receiving blanket is the perfect size. Its fabric should be lightweight and breathable. Try swaddling a few times when your baby is happy so that you're not struggling with a fussy or rigid baby—or try swaddling a doll, stuffed animal, or a friend's experienced baby first. Everybody's method is a little different, but here are the basic directions (see illustrations on the next page):

1. On a stable surface (such as a bed or clean floor), lay the blanket out in front of you so it's shaped like a diamond. Fold down the top corner. Place baby in the middle of the blanket with his head lying on top of the folded corner.

2. Hold your baby's right arm down against his body. Pull the left corner of the blanket across baby and over his right arm so that it's snug but not too tight. Tuck this corner under his body on the other side.

3. Bring your baby's left arm to his side, and bring the blanket's bottom corner up and tuck it under his left shoulder.

4. Pull the upper edge of the blanket down over his left shoulder, and bring the right corner across baby, keeping both his arms down against his body.

5. Pull the tail of the blanket around your baby like a belt, and tuck it in where it fits to prevent the blanket from unwrapping, or simply hold your baby or position him so it remains snug.

A veteran parent, a nurse, your doula, your lactation consultant, or your doctor can give you a swaddling demonstration if you can't seem to get it right. It can seem like a complicated process, but once you've seen it done a few times, you'll get the hang of it. And both you and your baby should enjoy the calming results.

Tips for Safe and Happy Swaddling

- When swaddling your baby, you'll want her toasty warm, not hot. To check your baby's temperature, slide your hand inside the swaddle to her chest and belly. She should feel comfortably warm, not hot or sweaty. Modify the thickness

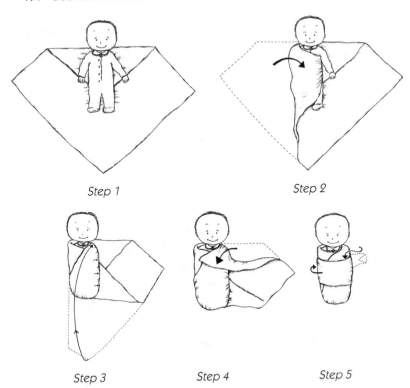

Step 1

Step 2

Step 3   Step 4   Step 5

and material of the swaddling blanket and the amount and type of clothing your baby wears under the swaddling blanket, or adjust the temperature of the room. On warm days, a diaper and T-shirt under a cotton blanket may be just perfect.

- Use a baby-sized receiving blanket or a specially designed swaddling blanket, such as one with Velcro ends or tabs that hold the blanket together.
- The blanket should fit snugly but not so tightly that it could impede circulation or breathing, prevent leg movement, or cause discomfort.
- Premature babies or those with developmental issues may need to have their arms up or free of the swaddling. Check with your health care provider about this.

- Protect your baby's hip and knee development by allowing ample space for his legs, or use a stretchy fabric that permits leg movement. Allow your baby to have a natural position for his legs when you wrap him; don't force them to be perfectly straight. Allow room within the blanket for your baby to stretch out his legs during sleep. If you aren't sure if your baby has enough leg freedom, try loosely double-diapering your baby before swaddling; this creates some extra space within the wrap and creates a natural flex to the hips. Some swaddling blankets are created with an opening at the bottom for complete freedom of leg movement.
- If your baby finds comfort in sucking his thumb or fingers, then swaddle him with one hand free, alternating hands each time you swaddle him. Some babies enjoy being swaddled with both hands untucked.
- Make certain that your swaddled baby is always positioned on his back for sleep.
- Don't allow the blanket to rise up to cover your baby's face or cheeks.
- Do not attach your swaddled baby to a cradle board for carrying, as this has been found to impede hip and leg movement necessary for proper development.
- If you swaddle your baby for sleep, be sure you unswaddle him when he is awake. Include plenty of supervised tummy time each day.

Father-Speak

"I'm amazed at how well swaddling her works for naps. It's ingenious. This has got to be one of the best ideas ever in the history of humankind. It's up there with the wheel and lightbulbs, if you ask me!"

—Khalid, father of two-month-old Aaliyah

When to Stop Swaddling Your Baby

Swaddling works well for babies from newborn until three to four months of age. However, babies who are used to being swaddled for naps may enjoy it for several months longer. It's time to wean from naptime swaddling when your baby

- is able to wriggle free of the swaddling blanket
- can roll over onto her side or stomach
- fights against you when you swaddle her
- no longer settles easily to sleep when swaddled

How to Wean from Swaddling

Many babies naturally outgrow their need to be swaddled. Every few weeks, test to see if your baby will accept napping without being swaddled.

Those babies who are reluctant to give up their sleeping swaddle can be weaned gently, a little at a time. The following ideas can help you set a plan for weaning from swaddling:

- Leave one arm unwrapped, then two arms, then both legs. You can experiment with this approach; take a few days or a week or more at each stage. Some babies respond better if you begin the weaning by leaving their legs undone first then progress to arms.
- Another weaning approach is to gradually loosen the blanket by increments over a period of days or weeks, allowing your baby a bit more movement. This way she remains swaddled but slowly gets used to having more freedom during sleep.
- When you finally stop swaddling, you might then dress your baby in a sleeping-bag-style sleeper or a wearable blanket. These create a feeling that is similar to being swaddled, but looser. After a while you can switch your baby to sleeper

pajamas with feet. Finally, over time, your baby can be covered with a blanket instead of being swaddled in it, if he prefers, though many toddlers still enjoy the freedom of wearing "footie pajamas" to bed.

- It can help to warm the crib sheets before naptime with a towel from the dryer, a microwaved heat bag, or a heating pad set on low. (Test the temperature of the surface before you lay your baby down.)

- Weaning from swaddling can be easier if you maintain all other parts of your baby's usual nap routine and when you keep other parts of the nap environment stable, such as darkening the room and playing lullabies or white noise.

- A newly unswadddled napper can sometimes be settled into bed if you place both hands on her (across her chest, stomach, or thighs) when you place her in the crib. When she is settled in place, then slowly reduce the amount of pressure of your hands until you remove them completely.

- If your baby has been sleeping well while swaddled but has outgrown the swaddle but not the need for assistance to nap, you might consider letting her nap in a cradle-swing, rocking cradle, or baby hammock. These can provide your baby with just enough physical stimulation to take over where swaddling leaves off.

- Your baby might welcome a small, soft lovey stuffed animal in the crib as a tactile replacement for swaddling. Look for a toy made especially for infants. Place this beside your baby's hips or legs.

- Continue to use white noise or soft music for naptime and maintain all the other parts of your baby's presleep routine.

Changing Car Naps to Bed Naps

....

See also: The Nap Resister: When Your Child
Needs a Nap but Won't Take One

> My son is a finicky sleeper and refuses to
> nap in his crib. I have resorted to driving around
> every day until he falls asleep, then I park in
> the garage and have to run in and out of the
> house to check on him until he wakes up.
> This is not only ridiculously expensive, but
> I'm really embarrassed and beginning to
> resent being held hostage like this
> every day. Help!

Oh, my! The things parents do to induce children to nap! I must tell you that you aren't the only one who has succumbed to driving a baby around town at naptime; it is surprisingly common. As effective as they are, the problems with driving naps are many. First, as you say, it's expensive and a misuse of resources and time. When you park your car and leave your sleeping baby unattended, it becomes a dangerous game of chance. You could be distracted and misjudge the amount of time between check-ins, and the possibilities of something bad happening while you are gone are endless: the temperature could become too hot and your baby could overheat; your baby could become twisted in his seat belt; or at the very least, he could wake up and panic at being alone.

When your baby becomes used to these driving naps, you'll find that they become a strong sleep cue—he'll fall asleep in the car even between naptimes, which can wreak havoc with your nap and bedtime schedule. The longer this pattern of driving naps goes on, the more ingrained becomes the habit, and your baby will come to connect naps and car rides and expect a chauffeured nap every single day.

The biggest problems with car-seat naps have recently been uncovered by several studies that show that spending too much time in this semi-upright position can put a strain on a baby's developing spine. In addition, spending awake time *and* naptime in the car seat, together with time in other baby carriers, increases a baby's chance of developing a flat area on the back of his head.

Other studies show that some babies (especially those who are newborn, premature, or sick) who take long, unsupervised naps in car seats appear to be at risk for breathing blockage or SIDS. Modifying car safety seats so that a baby's head does not flop forward could help avoid the risk, so keeping the seat in the back-tilted position (rather than sitting straight up) may be helpful. Installing the seat correctly, using the seat's belting system properly, and using specially made head-hugger inserts can also offset this risk by holding your baby in an upright position. (Read your manufacturer's instructions.)

Marjorie Marciano, director of the safety education office at the New York City Department of Transportation, offers this advice: "We do know that using a car seat that is installed correctly can reduce the risk of injury significantly, for example by 70 percent for children under one year old. 'Installed correctly' means that the seat should be at an angle of 45 degrees. When working with parents, we always say that it is important that the seat be at the correct angle to keep the airway open." This is a new discovery, and I suspect that car-seat designs will change in the future to offset this risk; there is more research needed here. In the meantime, it is prudent to avoid using your baby's car seat beyond the main purpose—car travel—for which the car seat remains the absolute safest place for your baby to be.

With older babies and toddlers, many parents allow the child to lie twisted, sideways, and even partially out of the car seat to recline against the door or a pillow during naps. This is another car-seat sleeping danger. In the case of an accident or a quick stop, the child could be ejected from the vehicle or suffer serious injuries because of the inappropriate location of the shoulder straps.

The bottom line is that driving your child to sleep in the car and letting him take his nap in the car seat is an unsafe and frustrating way for you to spend hours every day. The good news is that with some effort your baby can be taking long, pleasant naps—at home and even in his bed.

Why Are Car Naps Popular with Babies?

There are four main reasons that babies sleep well in the car:

- **W—Whooshing sounds:** The pleasant hum of the motor, the wind rushing by, the music on the radio, and the click of the windshield wipers and turn signal blinkers not only soothe your baby to sleep, they also block outside noises that interfere with a nap.
- **O—Orderly, predictable events:** Diaper changed, coat on, baby into the seat, buckle clicked, car started, driving begins, sleep time! It's exactly the same every single time—a very predictable and a memorable routine.
- **M—Movement:** Gentle sways, jiggles, and bumps create a pleasant rocking that puts babies to sleep.
- **B—Buckled:** Snapped snugly into her seat, your baby's own movements don't startle her awake. In addition, she isn't free to move around and evade sleep. She's snuggled into in a comfy, snug nest.

Car rides imitate a number of facets of the environment from the WOMB that babies find soothing and sleep inducing. The good news is that you can re-create this collection of sensations for your baby at home to create a new naptime routine. Choose some of the following tips for creating the sensation of a car ride at home.

W—Whooshing Sounds

The womb is a very noisy place, with the constant sound of a thumping, whooshing heartbeat. Babies become accustomed to these sounds, so a newborn may find a completely quiet room a bit disconcerting. You can help soothe your baby to sleep by adding sound to his sleep environment. The best sounds are sounds called *white noise*, such as the sound of waves, rainfall, or an air conditioner. There are a number of recordings and sound devices or clocks that play a variety of white noise options. You can even find recordings of car-ride sounds! Shop around and find something that your baby and you can both enjoy listening to. It is perfectly fine to have white noise running during your baby's entire naptime and nighttime sleep hours, as well.

O—Orderly, Predictable Events

At a very young age, babies come to rely on the familiar sequence of events in their day. They learn that getting undressed in the bathroom and the sound of running water means a bath is coming, for example. You can take advantage of this natural instinct by setting up a specific prenap routine. It doesn't have to be long and involved, and as a matter of fact, it shouldn't be—since your tired baby can get a second wind if your routine is too long. A few predictable actions will have your baby welcoming naptime. A simple routine might be diaper change, feeding, lights off, white noise, rocking, and to bed with a whispered "Night, night, sleep tight."

M—Movement

It's natural for children to be lulled to sleep with gentle movement, especially when coupled with white noise and preceded by a prenapping routine. There are many ways to provide movement for naptime, such as a giving your baby a cuddle in a rocking chair, walking him in a sling, giving him time in a baby swing or bouncy seat, or even gently jiggling or patting him as he lies in his bed. Experiment with the intensity and pace of the movement and see if you can use movement to relax your baby. Then place him in bed once he is nearly asleep, jiggling or patting him during the transfer, perhaps using the Pantley Dance (see page 144).

B—Buckled

If your baby is under five months old, the easiest way to create a snug sleeping cocoon is to swaddle him in a light blanket. For swaddling tips, see the information and diagrams starting on page 193. Some babies need to adjust to being swaddled if it is new to them, so give your baby a few opportunities to get comfortable with it before you abandon the idea.

Another way to re-create the snug nestlike environment of a car seat is to let your baby sleep in a smaller cradle or bassinet, or a baby hammock, rather than a large crib.

Changing the Habit Without Disrupting Naptime

There are a number of ways to approach changing your baby's nap routine gradually so that you don't create tears or disruption to your baby's naps. What follows are some ideas for making the change. You can pick one, or mix and match ideas to come up with the right solution for your baby. Stick with your plan for at least a week before you move on to something else, as it may take some time for your baby to adjust to the change.

Move Your Sleeping Baby

If your baby is a sound sleeper, transfer her to bed as soon as she is sleeping. Once she becomes accustomed to this, you can experiment with transferring her when she is sleepy instead of fully asleep. When you move her, stay slow and quiet and pat, rub, or jiggle her during the walk from the car to the crib, continuing the gentle motion until she is settled in the crib. (See "The Pantley Dance" on page 144.) If your baby is not used to sleeping in the crib, try putting a small travel bed or infant head and body sup-

Grace, five months old, in Daddy Jesse's arms

port cushion inside the crib to make it a bit more like the cozy snugness of a car seat.

Invest in a Crib Vibrator

Several companies produce devices to create motion in the crib. Some have a motor that attaches to the bottom of the crib and vibrates while it makes a whooshing sound. (One unit, the Sleep-Tight Infant Soother, was designed by a father who had a colicky, nonsleeping infant!) An Australian company produces the Lullabub, which consists of four canister-shaped modules that are placed under each leg of the crib and vibrate the crib with a gentle rocking motion.

These devices can be an effective way to turn the crib into an at-home car ride. As wonderful as any product may appear, there is no solution that works for every baby. So look for one that includes a money-back guarantee.

Let Your Baby Nap in a Cradle-Swing or Hammock

Babies who sleep well in the car will often accept a substitute location if it provides some of the sensory stimulation of the car ride, and a cradle-swing or hammock will do just that. These also create the slightly upright angle that is similar to a car-seat position so are particularly helpful for babies with colic, reflux, or respiratory issues.

It may take a week or so to make this adjustment if your baby is used to sleeping in the car; after all, you are changing a routine that your baby is familiar and happy with. It can help if you add the sounds of white noise, music, or a familiar station if the radio is typically turned on in the car. It may take some coaxing on your part, but a daily nap in the swing or hammock is much easier on you, and safer for your baby, than a car nap.

At some point you'll need to transition your baby to a bed, but many parents feel that a long, peaceful nap every day is worth it. When the time comes to change to stationary sleep, there are plenty of ideas in the chapter "Swinging, Bouncing, Vibrating, or Gliding: Making the Transition from Motion Sleep to Stationary Sleep."

Have Your Baby Take a Ride in His Crib

If your baby is hooked on sleep in his car seat, you can make a step-by-step transition to the crib. First, place your baby's car seat in his crib. Fold a small towel for under your baby's back so that he is lying less in a seated position and more horizontal. Turn on a white noise recording, tune the radio to a talk station, or play soft lullaby music. Dim the lights. Put a chair in the room for you, along with a book, a craft activity, or paperwork. Or set up your yoga mat or a tub of laundry to fold.

Once the room is set up, go through your normal routine, including picking up your car keys. Then, instead of going to the car, take your baby to the crib and belt him into the car seat. Sit beside the crib and slightly jiggle the seat. If he starts to fuss, place your hand on his belly and say, "shhh, shhh" while you jiggle the seat. Once your baby is settled and sleepy, experiment with reducing or stopping the jiggling. Leave the seat motionless once your baby is asleep.

To keep your baby safe, you *must* remain in the room during his nap. This is why you've set up a quiet activity for yourself. Leaving your baby alone like this could result in him tipping his seat over, becoming entangled in his belts, or slumping over in his seat.

After a few days or a week of this, you can begin to modify your baby's position so that he is less seated and more lying down. You can put a bigger towel under his back. Put a large book under the foot portion to tilt your baby to a more flat, level sleeping position. After a week or so, take the seat out of the crib and

Professional Words of Caution

- Children should never be left alone in or around a car whether they are in their car safety seats or not.
- Don't leave your baby unattended in a car safety seat, inside or outside of the vehicle.

—Recommendations from the
American Academy of Pediatrics (AAP)

put your baby to sleep directly in the crib. At this point you may want to put a portable travel crib, Moses basket, or baby positioner in the crib. By now, your baby has become used to the new routine and the new location and may welcome this new type of nap. If he fusses, place your hand on his belly or legs and softly shush him to sleep. Continue to use the white noise and dimmed room for every nap.

Avoiding Unplanned Car-Seat Naps

A busy day sometimes puts you and your baby in the car just before naptime, so your little one will easily fall asleep. If you try to move him after even a few minutes of sleep, he may wake up and stay up, bright-eyed and bushy-tailed! His short snooze will have "taken the edge off." Remember from Part 1 of this book that a five- to fifteen-minute nap takes your baby through the first two stages of sleep, which increase alertness and reduce homeostatic pressure, making it unlikely that your baby will fall back to sleep once you get him out of the car and up to bed.

To avoid a car-seat micro-nap, try to organize your outings to occur just after your baby wakes up in the morning or after he wakes up from a nap. Keep in mind that your baby's nap schedule changes over time, so watch for your baby's sleepy signals that tell you when he is ready to sleep. Next week's schedule may be different from today's.

Keep a backseat rearview mirror in your car so you can keep an eye on your baby. If you find yourself in the car and your little one looks sleepy, it's time to kick up the fun factor in the car: call out his name, ask a few questions in a lively voice, and even sing a cheerful, upbeat song. Then as soon as you pull the car up to your house, get your baby in for a nap before you even unload the groceries!

Changing Timing of Naps to Harmonize with Your Routine

There are times when your baby's naptime clashes with an unavoidable routine outing, such as picking up an older child from school. When this happens, you can slightly modify your baby's napping time since daily sleep is connected to other key factors that you control. The factors that you'll monitor, and then amend, are your baby's bedtime, mealtimes, and morning awaking time, to align better with your schedule.

Keep a journal for a day or two to track your baby's times of sleeping and eating. Once you've figured out a pattern, jot down what adjustment would be necessary to better coordinate with your daily car trips. Aim to shift everything by fifteen-minute increments until your baby is sleeping at a more convenient time.

Car Naps During Long Journeys

There will likely be times when you'll have a long drive and your baby will take a long nap en route. This is nothing to worry about. Just have a mirror set up so that you can keep on eye on your baby. When you can, break up a long journey so you can stop and take your baby out of his seat from time to time when he is awake.

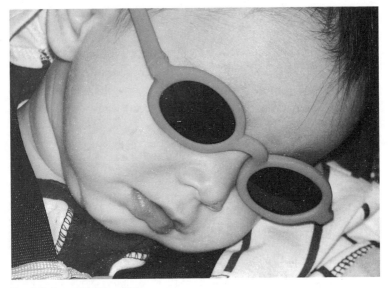

Daniel, four months old

Occasional Car Naps Are Acceptable

It would be impracticable to schedule your life around your baby's nap schedule, and it would be impossible to prevent a baby from *ever* falling asleep in the car. There will be days when a car nap is unavoidable. When that happens, try to let your baby nap for at least twenty minutes. If you wake her while moving her to bed, it is unlikely she'll fall back to sleep again, but at least you will have refreshed your baby enough to get through to the next naptime.

Colic Care

Helping Your Baby Get Comfort and Relief from Naps

My baby has colic. Every afternoon he gets
into a crying spell and cries nonstop for hours.
He rarely falls asleep during these periods,
and when he does, it is only for a short nap.
He gets severely overtired. What can I do
to stop the crying and help him sleep?

Colic is as hard on parents as it on babies. Their intense crying is heartbreaking and leaves parents feeling helpless and frustrated. Colicky babies, as this parent describes, have regular periods of inconsolable crying, typically late in the day. These bouts can last one to three hours or more and can definitely interfere with your baby's afternoon naps. What causes colic is still a medical mystery, so it can't be prevented. Without an exact cause, we can only focus on the methods that ease a baby's symptoms and help him relax enough to fall asleep. Studies tell us that sufficient daily naps can reduce the frequency and length of colic episodes and can help ease your baby's discomfort.

The exact mix of solutions that help a colicky baby nap are different for every baby, and parents are unique in the methods that they wish to use. Experiment with the various ideas until you find the right combination that works for you and your baby.

Research Report

Colic experts from the University of London's Institute of Education discovered that a shortage of overall sleep hours increases periods of fussing and crying for colicky babies.

Things That Ease Crying and Help Your Baby to Nap Better

Remember that nothing you do will eliminate colic *completely*. That will happen only when your baby's system is mature and able to settle on its own. However, when you can reduce your baby's crying, you will enable him to take better naps, which will lessen the effects of colic.

Look for patterns to your baby's crying; these can provide clues as to which suggestions from the following list are most likely to help your little one. Try not to overwhelm your baby or yourself with too many changes at once. Watch for any signs of improvement when you try something new. If the particular course of action doesn't change anything, don't get discouraged—just try something else until you find tips that work for you and your baby.

- Watch your baby for signs of tiredness and put her to bed the moment she appears sleepy. If you have a hard time reading your baby, refer to the chart on page 8, which shows the typical amount of time a baby at this age stays awake between naps. Put your baby down for a nap *just before* you think she needs it.
- Hold your baby in a semi-upright position for feeding and directly afterward.
- Experiment with how often and when you burp your baby.

- Offer meals in a quiet setting free from distractions. Maintain the quiet mood for about thirty minutes after feeding.
- If you are breastfeeding, feed your baby on demand (cue feeding), for nutrition as well as comfort, frequently throughout the day.
- If you are bottlefeeding, offer more frequent but smaller meals; experiment with different formulas with your doctor's approval. Try different types of bottles and nipples that prevent air from entering your baby as he drinks.
- If your baby likes a pacifier, offer him one for naps and during fussy periods. Sucking on a pacifier increases the amount of saliva your baby produces, and the extra lubricant in his system can sometimes reduce the amount of gas produced.
- Invest in a baby sling or carrier and use it often during colicky periods.
- Put your baby in a stroller and take a walk. When the weather is unpleasant, bring your stroller in the house and walk your baby around at naptime. When he falls asleep, park him near you so that you can keep an eye on him.
- Give your baby a warm bath before sleep if this relaxes her.
- Place a warm towel or wrapped water bottle on baby's tummy (taking caution that the temperature is pleasantly warm but not hot).
- Dress your baby in clothes that are loose around the tummy area.
- Hold your baby with her legs curled up toward her belly.
- Massage your baby's tummy or give him a full massage.
- Swaddle your baby for naps. (See the chapter "How to Use Swaddling for Naptime" for information about swaddling.)
- Lay your baby tummy down across your lap and massage or pat her back.
- Hold your baby in a rocking chair or put him in a cradle-swing. (See swing information on page 174.)

Mother-Speak

"I invested in a cradle-swing as soon as I realized my baby had colic, and it saved my life. Before the swing, I had to carry and jiggle my baby for every nap, and my arms were falling off! The swing provides enough movement and sound to allow my baby to sleep."

—Barbara, mother of four-month-old Zoë

- Invest in a baby hammock, which gently cuddles and sways a baby to sleep.
- Look into a vibrating infant seat or cradle. The gentle vibrations can soothe your baby, and some professionals feel that they can also dislodge gas bubbles.
- Walk, sway, or jiggle with your baby in a sling in a quiet, darkened room while you hum or sing. Or put in a movie and pace the room while watching. Your baby will get his nap, and you can get in your daily exercise and a movie, too!
- Ask your health care provider about the various baby positioners and crib wedges that keep baby nestled and his upper body slightly elevated. If gas or reflux is at the root of your baby's colic, this may bring some relief.
- Try keeping your baby away from highly stimulating situations (loud noises, crowds, action) during the day when possible, especially in the half hour before each naptime. This will prevent sensory overload, which can increase the crying.
- Studies have linked secondhand smoke with an increase in colic symptoms, so don't allow anyone to smoke in the house, in your car, or near your baby.
- Take a rest yourself. Lie on your back and lay your baby on your tummy or chest. The rise and fall of your breathing

and your heartbeat are very soothing to your baby. (Transfer your baby to his bed if he falls asleep. Or do this in a room with another adult who is awake and can keep watch while the two of you sleep.)

- Investigate the use of a crib attachment that vibrates and hums, duplicating the sensation of a car ride.
- Play soothing music or turn on a white noise recording (such as womb heartbeat sounds, ocean waves, or rainfall).
- As a last resort, ask your medical care provider about medications or holistic remedies available for colic and gas.

When You Should Call the Doctor

Anytime you are concerned about your baby, call your medical care professional. In the case of colic, be sure to make that call if you notice any of the following:

- Your baby's crying is accompanied by vomiting, pain, or fever.
- Your baby is not gaining weight.
- Your baby is over four months old, yet the colicky behavior persists.
- Your baby doesn't want to be held or handled.
- The crying spree isn't limited to one bout in the evening, but on and off all day.
- Your baby does not have regular bowel movements and wet diapers.
- Your baby's crying is making you angry or depressed, which could mean that you have postpartum depression.

Special Situations

Questions and Answers

Day Care Snoozing: Napping Both at Day Care *and* at Home

My baby rarely sleeps more than thirty minutes twice a day at day care, and some days she won't nap at all. She gets exhausted and falls asleep in the car on the way home and then is difficult to get to sleep at night. Ironically, my best friend, whose son is at the same day care, has the opposite problem! He naps well at day care but not at home. It is very frustrating for both of us, and we don't know what to do.

When a child has two totally different environments in which to nap, unique problems can crop up. There are times when the two places are out of sync when it comes to nap routines, resulting in great naps at home and nap problems at day care or vice versa. Sometimes, the ever-changing situations cause poor-quality naps at both places, resulting in a sleep-deprived, fussy child.

Frequently, there are one or two aspects of the nap routine that make it work in one place but are missing at the other. For example, you and your child care provider may both rock your baby to sleep, but you pat her tummy and shush her when you lay her in bed, while your day care provider lays her down without the rub or shush, which are important parts of your baby's falling-asleep routine.

For older babies and toddlers, the day care situation can *encourage* naps—when other children are resting, your child will go along with the group. Conversely, a day care setting can *prevent* naps if your child is too stimulated and excited to sleep.

Another potential issue is that your child's schedule might be quite different on day care days versus at-home days. Perhaps a different wake-up time, different mealtimes, and more or less active playtime are causing nap inconsistencies.

So, the first step is to look carefully at home naps and day care naps and pinpoint the differences. The following chart can help you to identify these differences. If you aren't sure of the answers for the day care column, you can copy this page and ask your day care provider to fill in the answers.

Question	At Day Care?	At Home?
What time does your child wake up in the morning?		
Are there exact daily nap times?		
Is there outside playtime early in the day?		
What happens in the thirty minutes before naptime?		
Does your child watch television or movies in the hour before naptime?		
Where does your child sleep?		
Is the room dark or light?		
Where are doors and windows in relation to your child's sleeping place? Are windows covered? Are doors open or closed?		
What kind of noises can be heard from the sleeping area?		
Is there music or white noise?		
Does your child sleep with a toy or stuffed animal?		
Is the room warm or cool?		
How does the *nap* environment and routine differ from the *bedtime* environment and routine?		

Once you've analyzed the nap situation at both locations, you can pinpoint the differences and work to make the situations more similar. Let your day care provider know that you have concerns about your child's napping, and request a meeting. Talk over the issues and brainstorm possible solutions. A quality provider will work with you to come up with a plan and communicate ongoing results with you. In addition to the chart, look over the following list of ideas as you create your nap plan.

- Ask if your provider is open to a napping location other than the crib. Perhaps they have a cradle or baby hammock they can use, or maybe a willing provider will carry your baby in a sling for a nap. (Check local rules and regulations.)
- If your child won't nap at day care, try scheduling a short nap as soon as you get home, as a "make-up nap." This might take the edge off and help transition your child from day care to the remainder of the day at home.
- If it is a bad napping day, put your child to bed early at night—thirty minutes to an hour earlier than usual. Simply go through your normal routine, but a bit earlier.
- Add white noise to naptime, both at home and at day care. This can help to mask distracting and possibly alerting noises and create a consistent sleep sound. Look into purchasing a small sound machine or travel alarm that has recordings of white noise such as ocean waves or rainfall. Place the sound machine in the same proximity to your child's bed in both places (such as under the foot of the bed). It is likely that the white noise will be helpful to other children in the room as well as to your own.

Standing Up in the Crib

Whenever I put my son in his crib for a nap, he immediately stands up. If I lay him back down, he's up again in minutes. I know he's tired, but he'll continue to do this until he's crying to get out of the crib.

This is a typical problem for babies who are just learning to pull themselves up to a stand, and they'll often do this at naptime and bedtime as well. Sometimes they'll pull up but be unable to get down, even if they want to! What's happening here is a testament to the incredible instinctual learning process that is built in to every baby. When they are learning something new, it becomes a near obsession until the skill is mastered. The good news is that this phase is usually short-lived. However, there are several things you can do to move things along.

- Make sure your child has plenty of opportunities to pull up during the day. Take him to the playground or create obstacle courses at home with tables and chairs so that your little one can cruise around the house. Invest in a toddler walker, which is a stable push-toy your child can use as he learns to walk.
- If it fits your schedule, take your toddler out for a stroller walk at naptime. Since he can't be standing up in the stroller, he'll likely fall asleep during your walk.
- Schedule plenty of active time from morning until about thirty minutes to an hour before nap, then slow down the pace before nap as time to wind down. If your child likes you to read to him, this is a good time for books. Quiet puzzles or other sit-still activities may help get your child ready for naptime.
- Stay close and help him back down whenever he's up. This can be tiring but effective. Once you have him back down,

though, don't simply walk away—that can be an invitation for another "up." Instead, take a minute and rub or pat your baby and see if you can help him relax so that he can sleep. Add some white noise or music, and make sure the room is darkened.

- Try putting your baby for a nap in sleeping-bag-style paja- mas. They will allow your child freedom of movement as he sleeps but are harder to stand up in.
- Consider saying bye-bye to the crib and getting a toddler bed or putting a mattress on the floor. Create a new nap- time routine and end it with a back rub or other relaxing nap inducer.

Weaning from the Naptime Pacifier

My daughter uses her pacifier for every nap. When should I wean her from this, and how do I do it?

New studies tell us that pacifiers may be a good thing for new- borns and infants, as pacifier use during falling asleep appears to reduce the risk of SIDS. But once your baby is beyond the infant stage, it may be time to think about weaning. Some pro- fessionals recommend weaning a baby from the pacifier by age one as a preventative measure, with the argument that the older the child gets, the more attached to the pacifier he will become. Others advise that in the absence of developing dental or speech problems, you can wait until your child is two or three years old, since you can then use reasoning along with an incentive chart or distraction.

Most professionals are less concerned about pacifier use if it is used only at sleep times and is not an all-day habit. In the end, the decision is yours. You know your child better than anyone else does; when no medical issues are involved, only you can accurately assess what role the pacifier is playing in your child's life and in her sleep, and how you can best wean her from it.

Here are a few ideas for getting the process going when you're ready to start weaning your child from pacifier use:

- Unless there is a specific reason you must take away your child's pacifier, it's best to do it slowly but surely. Try to choose a time when there are no other major changes happening in your child's life, such as the birth of a sibling, potty training, starting day care, or moving.

- It can help to begin by making the pacifier scarce during the day except during critical times, such as when your child is hurt or in bed for a nap. It can be easier to wean active daytime use first and sleep use second.

- Use distraction during the day. When your toddler asks for her pacifier, first try to distract her: sing a song, give her a toy, or go for a walk. Do something to get her focused on things other than her sucking urge.

- Gradually reduce your child's use by keeping the pacifiers in her bed. Some families have a "no pacifiers downstairs" or "only in your car seat" rule.

- Give your child an alternative to help soothe her when she feels upset or tired. A cuddle, special lovey, blanket, or favorite toy may comfort her instead of the pacifier.

- When it comes time to remove the pacifier from sleep times, establish new bedtime routines that are different from usual so that the cues for pacifier use aren't as evident. For example, if your child typically is rocked with a pacifier, move your prebed routine to the sofa instead. If she usually sucks during the bedtime story, offer a sippy cup of water or teething toy during reading time.

- If your child falls asleep with a pacifier in his mouth and then wakes crying for it during the night, you can wean him of this need by using Pantley's Gentle Removal Plan, described starting on page 162.
- Some older children embrace the idea of a "pacifier fairy." She, of course, collects pacifiers left under the pillow by children who no longer need them and leaves wonderful toys behind in their place.

Bye-Bye Bottle: Weaning from Naptime Bottles

My ten-month-old baby still falls asleep with his bottle. I have a feeling I should be weaning him from this, but how will I get him to fall asleep if I take it away?

Weaning from a bottle isn't only about a method of feeding. It's about saying good-bye to a part of babyhood, a comfort object, and very likely, an important piece of your child's sleep-time ritual. Because of this, weaning shouldn't happen suddenly. The cold-turkey approach may only confuse your child and make both of you miserable. A more loving and gradual process is easier on your child and on you, too.

Many people find that it is easier to wean from daytime bottles before sleep-time bottles because of the distraction of daytime activities and the available substitution of food and drinking cups. It's nearly impossible to wean your baby from his naptime bottle unless you also wean him from his bedtime bottle, as the bottle is a very strong aid for sleeping. The following tips may help when weaning your child from sleep-time bottles:

- Add a little water to each bottle you give to your baby for each nap and nighttime sleep over a period of weeks until it becomes 100 percent water. The water is less enticing than milk or juice, and your child will likely use it less, and when he does use it, it will be fine; there won't be any concern about tooth decay.
- Substitute a smaller bottle by switching to a four-ounce version or a fancy style that holds less fluid. Once your child is accustomed to the smaller bottle, fill it only three-quarters full, then half.
- Replace the bottle with a pacifier or teething toy.
- Try offering your child a cup at the times he normally would have a bottle, or give him both—use the cup for milk and the bottle for water.
- Provide your child with a snack and something to drink right before he gets ready for bed. If his tummy is full, he may be less interested in a bottle of milk or juice. Then at bedtime, offer a bottle or sippy cup of water only.
- Revise your bedtime routine so that you avoid the usual places and situations where your child usually has a bottle. For example, read bedtime stories in a new location, such as sitting on the sofa.
- Review the other sections in this book to be sure your baby's nap schedule is on target and for ideas on how to make naptime more inviting to your child.
- Be patient. Some children take longer to wean from bottles than others. It's not worth the battle if your child isn't taking naps and is suffering from this lack of sleep. If the issue becomes a frustration for both of you, take a few weeks or even a month off from the weaning effort and then try again.

Wakes Up Crying

> My son wakes up crying. It doesn't matter how quickly I get to him, he simply wakes up with a full cry—even when I'm in the same room! He settles down as soon as I pick him up, but I can't seem to avoid the immediate crying when he wakes up.

If your baby has a consistent nap schedule, sleeps a proper amount of time, and calms down as soon as you pick him up, this is nothing more than his sleep/wake personality. Some babies simply wake up with a cry, no matter what. It's their way of announcing that they are done sleeping.

There are three times when crying upon wakening signals something else:

- If your baby does not get enough sleep for nighttime or naps, it is likely that he is still tired and craving more sleep. If he wakes crying and is not easily comforted in your arms, he may be telling you that he's still tired. Try rocking him or using any of your usual going-to-sleep actions to see if he will return to sleep. Analyze his daily sleep compared to the sleep chart on page 8 and determine if you need to make changes to his sleep schedule.

- If crying upon waking is unusual for your baby, he may be telling you that he is hurting. An ear infection, difficult teething, stomach pains, or other problem may cause him to wake up crying. If the behavior persists, call your health care provider for advice.

- If your baby wakes suddenly and lets out a panicky scream or a fearful cry yet seems unaware that you are there, then he may be experiencing a *night terror*. This is a state that exists between sleep cycles where your child is still asleep and unaware of what's happening. He may thrash around, his eyes may be opened with pupils dilated, but he won't be seeing you. The best response to a night terror is to hold your child and try a gentle touch along with a series of comforting words and "shhh shhh" sounds. Your child may not respond directly to your calming efforts, but usually these episodes are over quickly and your child will be back to quiet sleep.

Vacations and Trips: Napping Away from Home

Our baby is finally settling into a nap routine, but we'll soon be going on vacation. What should we do about napping while we are gone?

There can be tremendous fun and memory-making when you travel with your child, but routines are usually disrupted. It's best to organize as much as possible in advance but then try to stay relaxed, accept changes, and go with the flow. You can get back to your routine once you return home.

Be proactive in making your trip decisions in regard to all the details, including sleep-related issues. Review the following questions to help make good sleep during your trip more likely.

- Does your child sleep well in the car? If yes, plan your travel time to coincide with a nap or bedtime so your child can sleep through part of the journey. If not, plan to leave immediately after a nap or upon waking in the morning. Don't fool yourself into thinking your child will behave differently from the way he usually does. Dress him comfortably, take off his shoes, and give him a blanket. He'll likely fall asleep to the hum and vibration of the ride. If you have a finicky sleeper, plan your trip during the daytime hours and bring along plenty of toys and activities to keep your child happy.

• Is it necessary to make the trip all at once, or can you break it up with stops along the way? The longer your child is strapped in her seat, the more likely she'll become fussy, and the less likely she'll sleep when you need her to. Planning a few breaks can give her the exercise necessary to bring on tiredness. If you're on a long airplane or train voyage, use the hallways for walks.

• Do you have everything you need to make sleep during the trip possible? Items such as:

—window shades to create a darker, nap-inducing atmosphere

—a cooler for cold drinks; a bottle warmer if needed

—your child's favorite blanket, pillow, stuffed animals, and pajamas

—music, lullabies, or white noise on tape or CD

—a rearview car mirror to keep on eye on your child (unless a second person will be sitting with your little one)

—books to read to your child

—adult books on tape or quiet music to play during the times when your child is sleeping

—a battery-operated night-light or flashlight if you'll be traveling in the dark

Once You Arrive: Sleeping in an Unfamiliar Place

Preparation is the key to the tricky issue of getting your child to nap in an unfamiliar place. Obviously, you can't use the exact routines that work for you at home, but you can follow much of your usual routine and create a *similar* sleep setting for your child. If your little one sleeps in a crib, for example, you may want to bring along a portable folding crib. (Let your child sleep in it at home in advance so that it's familiar.) Bring along your child's blanket, crib sheets, pillow, stuffed animals, lullaby tape, or white noise clock. Pack a night-light to make middle-of-the-night potty runs and diaper changes easier, and so you can avoid turning on bright lights at night and disrupting sleep cycles. Your night-light can also be using during the tucking-in process.

For co-sleepers, your first order of business is to create a safe sleeping place for your child. Check out the room where you will be sleeping. If you know that pushing the bed against the wall or replacing a fluffy comforter with a blanket would make the situation safer, then politely explain that to your host. Let her know that you'll move things back before you leave (and then remember to do so). If you're staying in a hotel, the housekeeping staff will often help with this if you ask.

Remember that many daily cues help keep sleep consistent. Serving meals of familiar foods at regular times, exposing your child to daylight in the morning while keeping things dimly lit at night, and avoiding prebed wrestling matches can all help to keep bedtime and sleep time more natural.

Traveling the Zones: What to Do About Jet Lag

Traveling with a child can be a challenge because of the disruption to the daily routine, the excitement of activity, plus anxiety over meeting new people and adjusting to new surroundings. When you add a leap across time zones, you complicate matters even more, since your child's biological clock, which tells him when to feel awake and when to feel tired, is forced out of sync with the clock on the wall. Because of this, the very first and most important rule is to be flexible and patient! A few other tips may help your child overcome jet lag more quickly.

- Keep your child well hydrated with plenty of water, milk, juice, or breastfeeding sessions. Provide plenty of healthy, nonsugar snacks.
- Don't use any over-the-counter products designed for jet lag without your doctor's specific approval and instructions. Many of these can be harmful to young children.

- Switch to the new time once you've arrived at your destination, or on the trip over. Powerful biological cues, such as the timing of meals and naps, will help all of you adjust to the change in time more quickly.
- Avoid letting your child take long naps at the wrong times. This will prolong the adjustment. Keep naps to their regular length and wake your child gently. Typically, the excitement of the new environment will ease him out of sleep.
- Watch the time. It's easy to miss mealtimes, naptimes, and bedtime when you're on vacation. However, if you stick to your child's usual pattern, you'll be able to avoid any major meltdowns from a hungry, overtired child.
- Keep in mind that no matter what you do, it will take a few days to find a new rhythm. Don't overschedule your first few days, if possible.

Twins, Triplets, or Children Close in Age: Getting Two or More to Sleep

I'm the mother of five-month-old twins. I've finally gotten their night sleep somewhat under control, but their napping is all over the place. What can I do to get them napping better?

Having a dependable nap routine and consistent naptimes is important for all children but can be especially important for parents of multiples, who are dealing with more than one little personality. The basic nap rules apply as they do to all children, of course. Here we'll touch on the unique issues for parents of multiples.

Where Should They Sleep?

Together, apart, same room, different rooms, parent's room? There is not one right answer. Experiment a bit and do what feels right to you and what works best for your children. Be open to different sleep arrangements for nap versus bedtime, too. And don't be surprised if this changes over time. It's fine to make adjustments as you go.

Mother-Speak

"What we found is that things change from time to time and have since the girls were newborns. At one point, the girls will sleep together well; then they won't, so we separate them. Then, after a time, we start finding them in bed with each other again. My suggestion would be to have the most flexible furniture and room setups so that you can made necessary modifications throughout these transitions."

—Shahin, mother of six-year-old twins, Aria and Rose

Synchronizing Nap Schedules

Each child has individual sleep needs, and to a certain extent you can't force them to adapt to a schedule just because it would work better for you. However, the good news is that overall most children have similar sleep needs at similar ages, and this can work in your favor.

In order to guide your children toward the same napping schedule, make your best effort to coordinate all aspects of their daily schedules. They're more likely to accept the same nap time if they wake up, play, and eat at the same time. You can also encourage them to have the same sleep schedule by keeping their room dark during sleep times and brightly lit upon awakening and by utilizing white noise as a sleep cue and a way to mask outside sounds that could wake them.

Try to keep your children's energy levels in sync. Make sure that mornings are bright and that they have plenty of active, energetic playtime together. When it is nearing naptime, dim the lights, turn on soft music, and orchestrate a brief quiet playtime to transition from action to rest time.

Special Needs, Special Naps

Our daughter has special needs that complicate her sleep issues. How can we apply what we're learning in this book to our situation?

While sleep issues are common among all children, those with special needs are even more likely to have sleep difficulties, yet they definitely benefit from a consistent nap schedule. Since naptime is critically important to keeping your child's energy level up and keeping his mood and behavior stabilized, it's worth the time and energy to solve any nap problems. There are, of course, a wide range and various degrees of special needs, and therefore it may be helpful to converse with your health professional and parents of children with similar situations. No matter your situation, there are a few general guidelines that will apply to most families when it comes to addressing sleep issues.

- **Define your child's napping issues.** Take the time to complete the logs and worksheets provided in Part 1. These will help you understand how your child is sleeping and will assist you in the process of identifying the napping issues that need to be changed.

Many sleep problems are not at all related to your child's special needs, so keep in mind that nap problems are common among all children.

- **Make a realistic, thoughtful plan.** As you put together your sleep plan, be realistic and patient. Aim for a few short-term goals, and as you achieve these, set a few more.

- **One step at a time.** You may have a number of sleep issues that you'd like to change. Trying to fix everything at once may be overwhelming to you and your child. It may be more productive and less stressful to pick one or two issues and work to change those before moving on to the next. You can either pick the problem that bothers you the most or choose the one that may be easiest to correct. Once you've had success with one issue, move on to the next. Keep in mind that gradually applying all that you've learned in this book will bring the best long-term success.

- **Focus on routines and rituals.** Your child may respond best when all her daily activities are choreographed to occur in the same way and at nearly the same time every day. The predictability of routine not only provides your child with daily cues, but it also helps to set her biological clock so that she's tired when naptime comes, sleeps well, and wakes up refreshed.

- **Ask for help if you need it.** There are times when nap problems are due to sleep disorders that won't improve until they are resolved. If you've made a nap plan and followed it consistently for several months without any positive results, then read over the chapter "Could It Be a Sleep Disorder? When to Call a Doctor" to determine if your child might be served by a professional who can provide a more extensive evaluation and specialized remedies.

Adjusting to Family Changes: Divorce, Moving, Day Care, New Sibling, Sickness, and Other Life Events

We're expecting a new baby and will be moving to a new home soon. How can I protect our toddler's napping routines through all of the upcoming changes?

Any major family change is likely to interfere with your child's nap routines. The combination of stress, heightened emotions, disrupted schedules, and unfamiliar routines can wreak havoc on even the best napper's sleep. There are a number of things that can help your child settle into any new life situation.

- Thoughtfully approach the changes to your child's routine; don't just let things happen and get swept along.
- Maintain as much of your child's original routines as possible. Consistency will help make other changes easier to adapt to.
- Delay any additional changes, such as weaning, potty training, or moving to a toddler bed, until life has settled into a comfortable new pattern.
- Create familiar environments wherever your child sleeps. If the change is due to a move, the organization of two separate households, or the start of day care, try to make your child's napping place in the new location resemble as closely as possible her original location.
- Write down your child's naptime and sleep plan. Request that all caregivers approach naps in the same way whenever possible. The more consistency there is from place to place, the more quickly your child will adapt to necessary changes.

- Encourage your child's attachment to a lovey, such as a blanket or stuffed animal. Having a lovey will give your child a feeling of security no matter where he is.
- Be patient. Your child may have an adjustment period of several weeks, a month, or even longer, especially if she is sensitive to changes. Some extra one-on-one attention and a few more daily cuddles can provide just what she needs to feel comfortable and to get settled into new patterns.
- Once things have settled back to normal, review your nap routines and adjust them as needed to create an updated plan. Consistently follow your plan each day.

Daylight Saving Time

We're about to change our clocks for daylight saving time. I know it's only an hour, but the change seems to upset our routine for weeks. When it comes to my children's nap and bedtimes, what's the best way to deal with the time change?

You're not the only one to struggle with the sleep change that accompanies daylight saving time. About 70 percent of people find that their sleep schedule is off for a while after the time adjustment. The resetting of our watches disrupts our physical rhythm—since you can't push a button to change your biological clock.

Lessening the Impact of the Daylight Saving Time Changes

It can help simply to know that it's normal to take a week or even longer to adjust to the time change. Even if you use the suggestions that follow, have patience with yourself and your children until your biological rhythms catch up with the clock on the wall. Here are a few things that can help you make a quicker adjustment:

- Take advantage of the power of light and dark to reset your body clocks. Keep the house dimly lit in the hour before bedtime and use bright lights for the first hour after you wake up in the morning.
- If you have to put your child to bed an hour earlier before he's actually tired, extend your prebed massage or reading time. Either of these can help a child calm down and feel drowsy.
- Just because the clocks officially change at 2:00 A.M. doesn't mean you have to change yours at that time. Instead, change your clocks midafternoon before the time actually changes. That way you'll have made part of the adjustment to the new time before it actually comes into effect. You'll have adjusted your child's nap and evening meal to the clock, which will help the bedtime adjustment flow more smoothly.

If the Time Change Wreaks Havoc in Your Home

If you and your child are having lots of sleep problems already and the change in time makes things much worse, see if you can split the hour difference into fifteen-minute increments over four or more days up to the actual time change. If you have appointments or older children to pick up from school and sports activities, you can't actually change your clock. But, since babies and young children can't tell time, you can simply write down the bedtimes for the week in advance and just begin your bedtime routine at the adjusted time each night.

Could It Be a Sleep Disorder?
When to Call a Doctor

**I have tried every tip in the book, but my child
still won't nap, even though it is clear she
needs to! Are we doing something wrong,
or could our child have a sleep disorder?**

It is possible that a sleep disorder is at the root of your problem, and there are ways to make that determination. Before we discuss the symptoms of sleep disorders, contemplate the answers to these questions:

- Have you created and followed a clear, specific nap plan?
- Have you considered the exact problems and accurately targeted your solutions?
- Do you feel that you've been consistent following the plan you've created?

If you answered "yes" to all of the above, and despite all this your child continues to have sleep-related problems for both naptime and bedtime, it is possible that there is an underlying sleep disorder or medical reason that your child isn't sleeping well. About 10 percent of children have a true sleep disorder, and their sleep problems cannot be solved without it being identified and treated. However, when a sleep disorder is correctly identified and treated, children can get the sleep they need.

Signs That Your Child May Have a Sleep Disorder

The following is a list of symptoms that are associated with the more common sleep disorders. These might also indicate a heath problem, such as asthma, allergies, or reflux; plus, these conditions can create or exacerbate sleep problems. A review of these indicators can help you decide if you should seek medical advice about your child's sleep. It is possible that these symptoms will show up during nighttime sleep and not during short daytime naps but that the quality and quantity of naps may be negatively affected. Determine if any of these apply to your child:

- Snores loudly or snores almost every night
- Is a very restless, noisy sleeper
- Often breathes through the mouth during sleep
- Chokes, snorts, gasps, wheezes, or holds his breath in his sleep
- Has a persistent night cough
- Frequently has trouble falling asleep even when tired
- Wakes up every hour or two during the night
- Appears to be tired or lethargic even after a good night's sleep
- Sweats heavily during sleep
- Has frequent and intense night terrors or nightmares
- Sleeps in strange or contorted positions
- Frequently wakes up with a headache, heartburn, or sore throat
- Has a nasal sound to his voice and regularly breathes through his mouth
- Is difficult to awaken even after a full night's sleep or remains groggy for a long time after waking up
- Sometimes experiences muscle weakness when highly emotional (during laughter or crying)

- Is often inattentive, irritable, depressed, or hyperactive during the day
- Falls asleep often in front of the TV, at playdates, or at school
- Doesn't improve no matter what solutions you try, and your child's sleep problems have become almost unbearable for you to handle

Research Report

A common tip shared by parents is that a dose of allergy medicine, cold medicine, or antihistamines can help a child sleep better. According to scientific studies, these medications are no more effective in aiding sleep than a placebo. Worse, giving a child unnecessary medication can cause dangerous side effects that are not worth the risk.

Sleep experts agree that medication should be a last resort and a rarely used solution. "Drugs don't get to the root of the problem, the reason why the child isn't sleeping," says Raymond Sturner, M.D., Associate Professor of Pediatrics at Johns Hopkins University School of Medicine.

Solutions for Children with Sleep Disorders

If you suspect that your child may have a sleep disorder, it is best not to attempt to diagnose the problem yourself. There are a number of places where you can find help determining if your child has a sleep disorder. These professionals can also assist you in mapping out a treatment plan. Depending on your child's issues, your family's approach to health care, and the results you have along the way, it may take visits to more than one of these professionals to

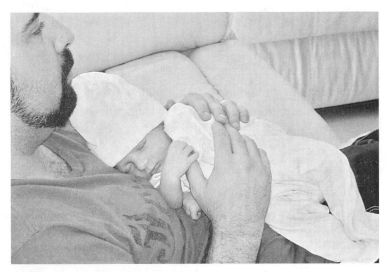

Daniel, one month old, on Daddy Gary

settle on the best answer. But don't give up. This is an important issue to solve for the sake of your child's health and well-being.

- **Your general health provider.** The pediatrician or health care provider who handles your child's regular checkups may be able to help you determine if a sleep disorder exists, what treatment to use, and if your child should see a specialist.
- **A sleep disorders center.** Specialized sleep centers are set up with the equipment necessary to perform diagnostic tests and sleep studies. Look for a center that specializes in pediatric sleep disorders if possible. You can acquire information about sleep centers from your local hospital or your health care provider.
- **Alternative medicine.** If alternative medicine options suit your family's approach to health care, many are able to effectively treat sleep problems. Some of the choices are as follows:
  —**Holistic medicine and homeopathy** will take into account your child's temperament, eating habits, prior illnesses, and family health history to determine which remedy and lifestyle changes would most improve your child's sleep situ-

ation. Homeopathic remedies are numerous and are made from minerals, plants, and animals.

—**Naturopathy** is an integration of natural medicine with medical diagnostic science.

—**Chiropractic care** focuses on treating health problems by making adjustments to the bony framework of the skeleton, particularly the spine. Chiropractic doctors can diagnose sleep disorders and deliver treatments for a better night's sleep.

—**Acupuncture** is a natural therapy that is used to heal illness and improve well-being. Acupuncture can be useful for the treatment of some sleep disorders.

—**Craniosacral therapy (CST), craniopathy, and cranial osteopathy** are holistic therapies that focus on the skull and the membranes and fluids that surround the brain and spinal cord. You may want to talk with your health care provider about looking into this option and locate a doctor who specializes in using this method for children.

• **Pediatric psychologists and family therapists.** Mental health professionals can often help to diagnose sleep problems and recommend treatment.

Choosing the Right Answer

Every family approaches health care in its own unique way. Whatever way you choose to handle your child's sleep problems, make sure that you take the time to investigate your choice thoroughly. When you select a method of care, give it enough time to work before evaluating your results. Sleep disorders are rarely corrected in one day, or even one month. These take time, care, and patience to remedy, but you may be providing your child a lifelong benefit by taking the necessary time to solve his sleep problems.

Index

About the Author

Parenting educator Elizabeth Pantley is president of Better Beginnings, Inc., a family resource and education company. Elizabeth frequently speaks to parents at schools, hospitals, and parent groups around the world. Her presentations are received with enthusiasm and praised as realistic, warm, and helpful.

She is a regular radio show guest and is frequently quoted as a parenting expert in newspapers and magazines such as *Parents*, *Parenting*, *American Baby*, *Woman's Day*, *Good Housekeeping*, and *Redbook* and on hundreds of parent-directed websites. She publishes a newsletter, *Parent Tips*, which is distributed in schools nationwide.

Elizabeth is the author of these popular parenting books, available in twenty-six languages:

The No-Cry Discipline Solution
The No-Cry Sleep Solution
The No-Cry Sleep Solution for Toddlers and Preschoolers
The No-Cry Potty Training Solution
Gentle Baby Care
Hidden Messages
Perfect Parenting
Kid Cooperation

Elizabeth is a contributing author to *The Successful Child* with Dr. William and Martha Sears.

Elizabeth and her husband, Robert, live in the state of Washington, along with their four children, Angela, Vanessa, David, and Coleton, and Grama (Elizabeth's mother). Elizabeth is an involved participant in her children's school and sports activities and has served in positions as varied as softball coach and school PTA president.

For more information, excerpts, parenting articles, and contests, visit the author's website at www.pantley.com/elizabeth.

More No-Cry Solutions

From trusted parenting author Elizabeth Pantley